21st Century Kitchens

Stephen Crafti

images
Publishing

Published in Australia in 2010 by
The Images Publishing Group Pty Ltd
ABN 89 059 734 431
6 Bastow Place, Mulgrave, Victoria 3170, Australia
Tel: +61 3 9561 5544 Fax: +61 3 9561 4860
books@imagespublishing.com
www.imagespublishing.com

National Library of Australia Cataloguing-in-Publication entry:

Author: Crafti, Stephen, 1959-
Title: 21st century kitchens/Stephen Crafti.
Edition: 1st ed.
ISBN: 9781864703764 (hbk.)
Subjects: Kitchens—Australia—Design
Dewey Number: 643.394

Edited by Chris Wyness

Designed by The Graphic Image Studio Pty Ltd, Mulgrave, Australia
www.tgis.com.au

Pre-publishing services by United Graphic Pte Ltd, Singapore
Printed on 140gsm GoldEast Matt Art paper by Millenium International Limited, Hong Kong
Printed in China

Contents

Introduction

IN THE VICTORIAN PERIOD, the kitchen, or scullery as it was referred to, was "back of house", or even located in a detached building. While the kitchen's status moved up a few notches over the next couple of decades, it never came close to competing with the formal rooms of the house—the kitchen retained the status of the tradesman's entrance.

However, following the Second World War, the kitchen became pivotal in the design of the house. In the 1950s, with the explosion of new kitchen appliances, the kitchen progressed to being a showpiece for modernity. New bright-coloured laminates started to appear, along with serviceable linoleums for kitchen floors. As anyone who has seen Jacques Tati's classic film *Mon Oncle* will remember, the owner of the modernist 1950s house proudly shows of her new kitchen, along with all the shiny new appliances, such as the pop-up toaster.

While the 1950s kitchen heralded a new wave of domestic modernity, it still remained separate from the informal living areas in the house. Even architect Harry Seidler's Rose Seidler House in Wahroonga, Australia (circa 1950), which in its day was the latest in contemporary design, separated the kitchen from the dining area. However, there was a service hatch, which allowed meals to be served into the adjacent dining area.

The 1960s saw a bridging of the kitchen and informal meals area. However, there was usually a bank of overhead cupboards in the kitchen that delineated the two spaces. For the housewife, who was generally relegated to the kitchen, the separation allowed meals to be prepared relatively uninterrupted. The family sat around laminate table settings eagerly anticipating their dinner, which more often than not consisted of a meat dish and three vegetables.

As women entered the workforce the division between the kitchen and the dining area became less defined. Rather than the kitchen being seen as a separate entity, it became integral to the informal meals area, and part of the open-plan living areas. In many cases the kitchen's central-island bench was the only room divider, and was also the hub of the home.

As this book illustrates, the humble kitchen has come a long way since Victorian times, and even since the 1950s. As well as being integral to large open-plan living areas, the contemporary kitchen often extends to outdoor living areas, be they a covered terrace, or even a second kitchen, complete with built-in barbeque and sink.

As people spend more time outdoors, either eating or simply relaxing, the focus of the kitchen has become the garden. Framed by picture windows and large sliding glass doors, the kitchen is designed to take advantage of garden views. Rather than locate the stove and hotplates against a blank wall, architects and designers consider the kitchen's aspect, as well as its connection to the living areas.

As was mentioned by many of the architects and designers who were interviewed for this book, the kitchen is one of the most challenging areas of the house to design. Understanding the way the kitchen is used by the family is often the starting point. "Each client has a unique way of cooking, and the kitchen must be tailor-made to them," says architect Franco Fiorentini, a co-director of F2 Architecture. Many others are conscious of the distances that need to be covered in the kitchen—from the fridge to the sink, hotplates and oven. With this in mind, spaces between facilities in the kitchen are finely measured, with a plan created to ensure ease of movement.

Being integral to open-plan living areas, the kitchen is becoming less obvious. While there are generous benches, storage is often concealed. Likewise, the fridge and pantry are often tucked away behind a door,

allowing the kitchen joinery to appear seamless. And what is significant in kitchen design is a trend towards a second and smaller kitchen. Complete with a sink, dishwasher, and additional storage and bench space, this kitchen or "butler's pantry" allows for the preparation of food without all the associated mess in the main kitchen area. Ideal for entertaining, the butler's pantry allows the kitchen to remain pristine, particularly when on view to the living areas.

Another recent trend is a move towards the use of sophisticated materials. Concrete poured in situ to create a kitchen bench creates a sense of solidity. And although laminates still continue to be popular, others prefer to use more refined and expensive materials such as American oak and cherry wood, once considered the domain of bedrooms and living areas. Materials that prove hardy and attractive, such as Corian and reconstituted stones, continue to be used. Not only is Corian attractive but, as shown in one kitchen, it can be used to create a seamless finish between benchtop and splashback. Other designers prefer to use marble in kitchens, but rather than use it indiscriminately it is sometimes added as a trim.

Choosing between laminate, timber, or marble in a kitchen will often depend on the materials used in the informal dining and living areas. Keen to create a fluid open space, one material is often carried through to the other areas in the house. Many designers include extensive drawers and cupboards in the central-island bench—on the kitchen side the bench features large sliding drawers for cookware, and on the dining-area

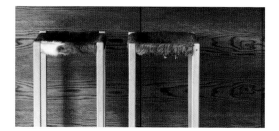

side there is an extensive bank of cupboards and smaller drawers for crockery and cutlery.

One of the most significant influences on modern kitchens is a shift towards alfresco dining. Rather than the formal dining area, once popular in the Victorian period, there is a preference for more informal dining. One architect, for example, designed a kitchen and meals area inside the house, but shortly after the project was finished the owners requested the addition of an outdoor pavilion adjacent to the kitchen. Rather than creating a separate area, the architect designed the kitchen bench to extend to the outdoors, complete with a sink, built-in barbeque, and additional storage. This new structure has reed-like walls and is covered with a polycarbonate roof for weather protection, and there's a retractable blind for protection from the afternoon sun.

Whether it's a free-standing pavilion, or a large timber deck that leads from the informal living areas, cooking is no longer confined to one particular space. Meals move easily from the kitchen to the outdoors. Rather than having the smell of meat linger in the house it's often preferable to cook on a barbeque, or in some cases use a wok in the outdoor kitchen. And to further enhance the experience of outdoor cooking, there are often veggie patches and herb gardens within easy reach of the chef.

There is a continuum of kitchen types in this book, from the sleek and expensive to the simple and more economical. However, what all these kitchens share is the desire to place the kitchen centre stage.

Projects

The house, with a
large open-plan
kitchen, living and
dining area, has a
strong warehouse feel

THE KITCHEN AND LIVING areas in this house are located on the first floor rather than at ground level. "We couldn't ignore this outlook," says architect Reg Lark, pointing out the ferries on Sydney's Manly Harbour. "The light is also greater on the first floor," he adds. The house, with a large open-plan kitchen, living and dining area, has a strong warehouse feel. With concrete floors and generous ceiling heights (varying from 3.5 to 4.5 metres), it has an industrial aesthetic. **>>**

1 Kitchen
2 Living area
3 Verandah

0   5m

One of the main features in the kitchen is a long central island bench, approximately 5.5 metres in length. Made of Corian, with large stainless-steel drawers below, it's the first port of call. "My clients love entertaining. A large island bench formed an important part of the brief," says Lark. The bench is complemented with a bank of timber-veneer cupboards. These cupboards conceal a microwave, fridge and pantry, as well as a storage area. To reinforce the industrial aesthetic, a stainless-steel splashback was included between the cupboards, which continues to form a benchtop. "The stainless steel was designed as one piece. There are no joins," says Lark.

In the kitchen, large glass stacking doors lead to the terrace, which is finished in concrete. Although the owners regularly dine on the terrace, they also spend considerable time sitting at the island bench. "I've positioned the bench so you feel half inside and half out," says Lark, who angled the ceiling 20 degrees to the terrace. "I wanted to maximise the views, as well as the light," he adds.

To further enhance a sense of the outdoors in the kitchen, and to open up the space as much as possible, Lark designed a series of aluminium slats in the roof, hovering below a glass skylight.

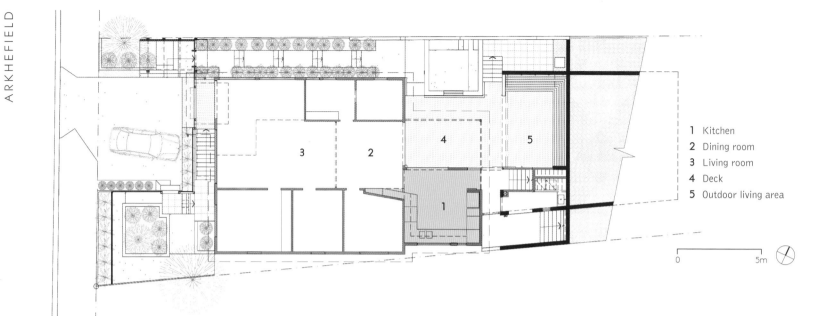

1 Kitchen
2 Dining room
3 Living room
4 Deck
5 Outdoor living area

0   5m

The double-height space allows views to the past and present

THIS TRADITIONAL QUEENSLANDER was only renovated five years ago, however, the previous renovation failed to connect the kitchen with the outdoor areas. Because it's quite a steep site there previously had been the feel of walking into a cave.

To change this experience, a new contemporary wing was added and the main entrance was relocated to one side of the house, making the outdoor areas to the rear more accessible. Past the period home, the owners now arrive to a covered terrace with a connected plunge pool. The double-height space, featuring 6-metre-high ceilings, allows views to the past and present, and a sense of transparency between the two styles. The outdoor terrace, which leads from the new kitchen, features a striking timber wall made of tallowwood, which continues on the ceiling. Tallowwood is an extremely hardy timber that with time will turn a silvery grey. To activate the outdoors, the architects included a feature wall made from ceramic tiles in hues from chocolate brown through to white. The clients have four children under five, so the architect wanted to create a large enough outdoor space for them to ride their bikes. >>

Large glass-and-timber doors separate the kitchen from the deck. Featuring white Corian benchtops, the kitchen also includes Tasmanian oak for the lower cupboards and painted MDF cupboards above. Separating the two is a glass splashback painted red. To bring in additional light, while maintaining privacy, there's an architecturally designed frosted-glass window. Given the age of the children it was important that robust materials were used, so linoleum features on the kitchen floor while the furniture on the terrace is made from plastic.

Although the family gravitates to the pool and deck, there is also a separate courtyard on the other side of the living room, complete with sandpit and barbeque.

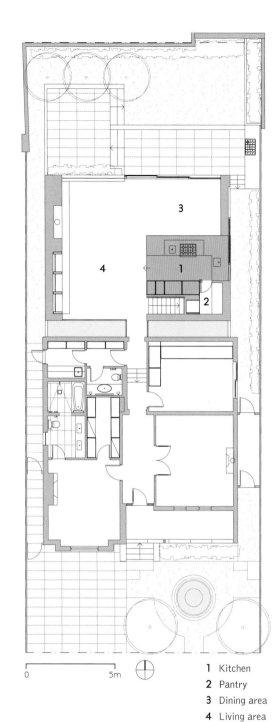

0   5m

1   Kitchen
2   Pantry
3   Dining area
4   Living area

While the location of the kitchen and living areas is unchanged, it has been separated from the period home by means of a new glazed breezeway

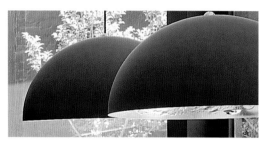

THIS DOUBLE-FRONTED VICTORIAN home wasn't quite large enough for the family that lived in it. Besides a shortage of bedrooms, the kitchen and living areas were disjointed, with several pathways crossing these areas. "The house was renovated only a few years ago. The kitchen was more than serviceable, but it didn't meet our clients' requirement. One of the owners loves to cook and entertain," says architect Andrew Piva, an associate with b.e. Architecture.

To create the extra space a second level was added, which is partially concealed behind the pitched roof. While the location of the kitchen and living area is unchanged, it has been separated from the period home by means of a new glazed breezeway.

The kitchen is considerably more integrated into the new wing. The only delineation between the kitchen and the living areas is a wraparound island bench made from reconstituted stone that sits on a slightly higher level. The kitchen is set down to create bench height to the working areas while maintaining table height in the adjoining dining room, thus making the back of the kitchen feel more like furniture. **>>**

A seamless transition between the kitchen and living areas was created by using reconstituted timber-veneer joinery in pewter-grey. Behind these kitchen cupboards are an integrated fridge and freezer, a walk-in pantry, an appliance cupboard and general storage. This wall of cupboards also conceals a staircase that leads to the first-floor bedrooms. One of the subtle divisions between the kitchen and dining area is a lowered range-hood, made from stainless steel. Task lighting, built into this rangehood, eliminates the need for pendant lighting.

Although the large sliding glass doors to the garden can be left open during the warmer months, the owners can also retract the sliding glass window in the kitchen overlooking a side courtyard. "We designed this window to allow it to disappear into a cavity wall," says Piva.

The most significant aspect of the kitchen design is its orientation to a raised garden

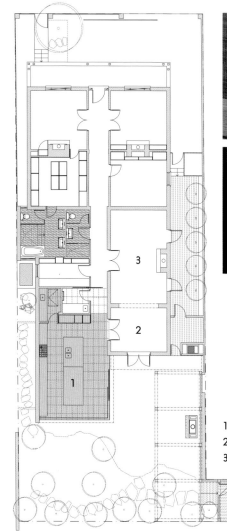

1 Kitchen
2 Dining room
3 Lounge

0   5m

THIS DOUBLE-FRONTED VICTORIAN home has been completed reworked by b.e. Architecture. While the formal front rooms of the house were retained, the later additions were removed. "The planning was wrong and the garden aspect was marginalised," says architect Andrew Piva, an associate with the practice. "We've extended the house further into the garden," he adds. A new kitchen and meals area extends across the entire width of the house, allowing for one generous space of approximately 5 by 8 metres.

The original part of the house features wide timber treads. Terrazzo tiles were used in the kitchen and living area to contrast the two periods. To create a synergy between the two periods, the architects designed the kitchen joinery with full-height cupboards made from reconstituted timber veneer and stained black-brown. This bank of cupboards conceals a walk-in pantry behind a large pivotal door, as well as the fridge and a storage area. "It reads as a feature wall," says Piva.

Another element in the kitchen is the oversized island bench. Made from timber veneer and bleached, the timber cupboards complement a white stone bench. One side of the kitchen bench includes a sink, dishwasher and an area for waste disposal, while the other side has storage for items such as crockery. The architects extended the island bench by adding a substantial timber table, also made from oak, that is not only used for all meals but also doubles as a place to catch up on some reading.

The most significant aspect of the kitchen design is its orientation via two walls of floor-to-ceiling glass to a raised garden designed to be ever changing with the seasons. The feeling within the kitchen area is almost as if the occupant is cooking 'plein air'. The colours of materials chosen are soft and understated letting the colours of the garden set the tone of the space.

When you're
designing a kitchen,
it's important to create
a sense of flow

THIS DOUBLED-FRONTED VICTORIAN home was endowed with bedrooms, but was short on living spaces. The original house also failed to connect with the garden. "We've transformed the place into a court-yard house," says architect Vanessa Bird, co-director of the practice.

The original four front rooms of the house were retained with the addition of a new kitchen, living and dining area, main bedroom and guest room. Featuring an oak-plywood curved ceiling, the dramatic arch appears to embrace the courtyard garden. "The ceiling was also designed for acoustics. The owners regularly have recitals," says Bird. >>

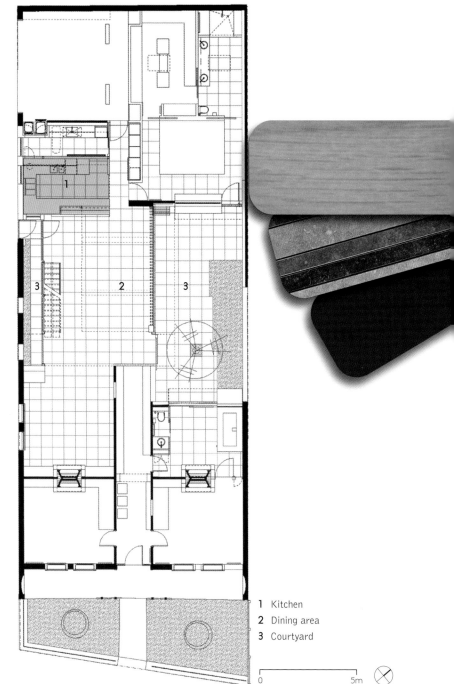

1 Kitchen
2 Dining area
3 Courtyard

0   5m

The kitchen, which forms part of the living areas, is nestled under the 'gallery' that frames the living area. "The kitchen is integral to the space, but it's slightly enclosed," says Bird, pointing out the raised oak shelves on the kitchen bench. Used for resting drinks, this bar also conceals dishes in the sink. "You don't want to see a failed soufflé from the dining room," says Bird.

On the side of the dining area, the kitchen's island bench also doubles as a credenza. Supported by a steel post and a block of oak, this unit with a black granite top is ideal for storing crockery. On the side of the kitchen, the benchtops are stainless steel, with joinery being a combination of two-pack black-painted cupboards and American oak cupboards. A separate walk-in pantry to one side of the kitchen is also included, and features a moveable trolley referred to as a 'baking station'. Piled with cake tins and a mixer, the trolley can be wheeled into the kitchen.

As the owners regularly move their grand piano around the living areas, the architects used porcelain on the floors in the kitchen, living areas and in the court-yard. According to Bird, it's not just the materials that should create a strong sense of connectivity, but the spaces themselves. "When you're designing a kitchen, it's important to create a sense of flow, allowing for fluid, rather than interrupted movement," she says.

A recent addition, a covered terrace with outdoor kitchen, has become a focal point for the family

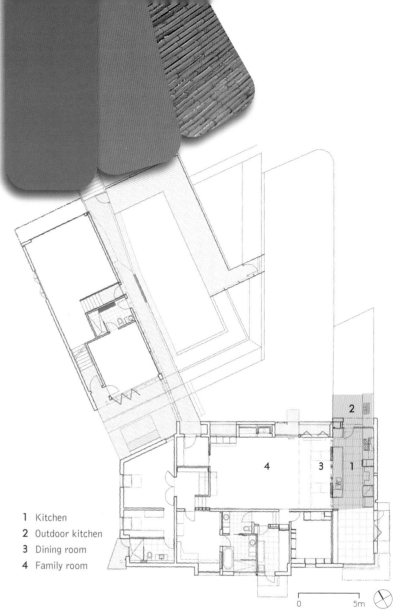

THIS FAMILY HOME INCLUDES a kitchen and meals area that can be opened up to the living areas or closed with sliding Ryegrass doors. "Most of the time, these doors are left open," says architect Vanessa Bird, who was keen to extend the kitchen views into a front garden.

The kitchen features Wenge cupboards in the Island bench, which is finished in Corian that extends on both sides. To one side of the kitchen is an informal meals area with generous floor-to-ceiling cupboards used for crockery and storage. There's also an ironing station concealed behind one of the cupboards.

A recent addition, a covered terrace with outdoor kitchen, has become a focal point for the family. The steel-framed pergola is clad in panels made from reeds. Hardy and weatherproof, these panels enclose the pergola on one side. "We wanted to filter the light as well as creating privacy from a neighbouring home," says Bird, who also included a roll-down blind on one side to eliminate the harsh afternoon sunlight.

1 Kitchen
2 Outdoor kitchen
3 Dining room
4 Family room

0   5m

While the indoor kitchen features the latest kitchen appliances, the outdoor kitchen includes a built-in barbeque and wok. Made from Corian, the kitchen benches, both inside and out, form a continuous line. To speed up the process of plating between the two kitchens, there's a canteen-style window to the terrace.

The family has the choice of eating indoors or out. "It's quite magical sitting on the terrace looking at the 'fabulous grass crescent' (a grass mound designed by Rush Wright Landscape Architects)," says Bird.

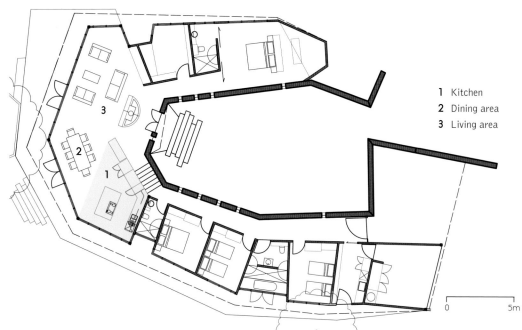

1 Kitchen
2 Dining area
3 Living area

Kitchens have to be robust. But they also have to tie in with the aesthetics of the rest of the house

THE FRONT DOORS OF this house open directly into this open-plan kitchen and living area. Accessed through a courtyard, there's an immediate sense of arrival. "The house was designed for a couple who love to cook and entertain. They wanted the kitchen to be a focal point," says architect Simon Knott, a director of BKK Architects.

Rather than locate the kitchen in a corner of the open-plan space, it is on display. "Traditional kitchens have the cooking appliances against one wall. But how can you turn your back on this view," says Knott, pointing out the rolling hills and sea in the distance. In this kitchen, the stove and hotplates are located in the L-shaped central bench. As well as the owners enjoying the views while cooking, they can also easily converse with friends and family seated at the dining table.

The kitchen joinery, like the timber windows, is dark charcoal. Made from MDF, the two-pack-painted joinery features a fluted textured surface. "We wanted to add depth to the joinery," says Knott, who included generous storage. A built-in pantry separates the kitchen from a stairwell. There's also a built-in appliance cupboard in the kitchen for everyday use.

Complementing the dark joinery are black concrete benches, formed in situ. "People are quite specific when it comes to kitchens. Sometimes, they'll come to us with an exact measurement between two areas of the kitchen," says Knott, who understands the specific nature of kitchen design. "Kitchens have to be robust. But they also have to tie in with the aesthetics of the rest of the house," he adds.

The kitchen and living areas are linked by generous glazing and rich timber flooring. Reclaimed from an old scout hall, the timber features nail marks from hundreds of years ago. "They add texture, as well creating a sense of history," says Knott.

A 1960S ARCHITECT-DESIGNED home was on this site originally, however, the only remnants of that house that remain today are two external walls. "We retained the original footprint and added a second level," says interior designer Sue Carr, of Carr Design Group. The house was the winner of the Residential Category at the 2009 Interior Design Awards. **>>**

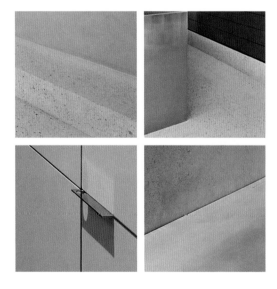

We wanted the house to breathe, as well as being connected to the garden

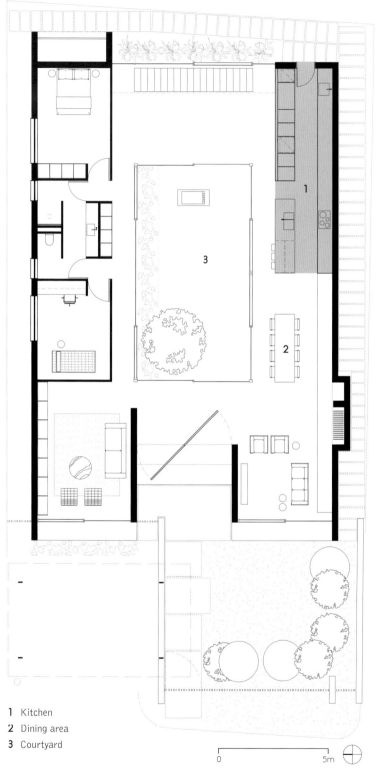

1 Kitchen

2 Dining area

3 Courtyard

0   5m

While the courtyard is in the same position as in the original home, the rooms surrounding it are considerably more open plan. "We wanted the house to breathe, as well as being connected to the garden," says Carr, who included large sliding doors to the courtyard and to the rear and front gardens.

The kitchen, dining, and informal sitting area occupy one wing of the house. With sliding glass doors at either end, as well as to the internal courtyard, there is a constant breeze. "The design responds to the prevailing winds. In summer, the house cools down relatively quickly," says Carr.

Rather than segment the kitchen from the dining and sitting area, the two areas are defined by means of a raised concrete plinth. In the kitchen the stainless-steel bench 'rests' on the plinth, while in the dining and sitting areas the plinth forms a hearth for a fireplace, as well as providing additional seating. "We didn't want the two areas to feel disconnected," says Carr.

While the steel bench, which includes the oven and hotplates, appears as a simple steel box, it conceals a pop-up splashback (also in stainless steel), and a pop-up screen that electronically controls functions in the house such as security and lighting. The island unit is designed in stainless steel – one side of the unit includes cupboards and a double sink, while the other portion forms a table that is ideal for casual meals.

To allow the courtyard to be used for cooking there is a concrete barbeque, complete with hotplates and grill. To unify the spaces, concrete floors appear inside and out. "It's a very simple design, but there's quite a lot of detail," says Carr, pointing out the fine shadow lines in the ceiling to conceal recessed lighting.

SITTING ON A 250-square-metre sliver of land, most of the original timber worker's cottage was retained while at the same time being completely transformed. "We kept the original structure, including the front verandah, for heritage reasons," says designer Carroll Go-Sam, who lives in the house with her partner and their two children.

We kept the original
structure, including
the front verandah,
for heritage reasons

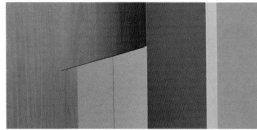

While the two front rooms of the original home were retained, and now used as bedrooms, an original low, rear skillion roof, which included the kitchen, was removed. As a response to the relatively compact site, it was decided to create a double-height space at the rear. At ground level the new steel-and-glass wing is the open-plan kitchen and living areas. Above is a mezzanine-style main bedroom and ensuite. "We wanted to 'explode' the space," says Paul Hotston, architect and director of Phorm Architecture + Design, who collaborated with Go-Sam. **>>**

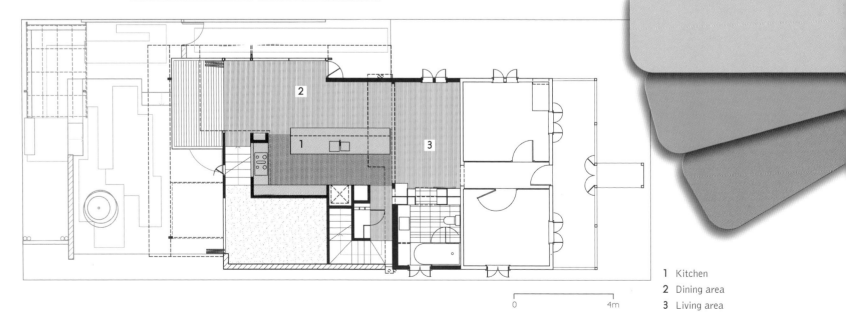

0   4m

1 Kitchen
2 Dining area
3 Living area

Central to the kitchen is a 4-metre-long island bench. Featuring a reconstituted-stone benchtop, the island bench functions as a preparation space, a place to dine and an area for the children to do their homework. To create the effect of a floating plane, the designer lifted the sides of the bench above the floor, "to contrast the heaviness of stone with lightness," says Go-Sam.

While the kitchen and combined-meals area are predominantly white, there are highlight colours throughout. The flooring, for example, is made from bamboo, the kitchen includes metallic-laminate joinery, which conceals a pull-out pantry, and there is a sea-blue-coloured glass splashback behind the hotplates.

Although the available space is compact, the volume of the kitchen creates a sense of openness. With generous glazing and operable pull-out windows, there's also a sense around the dining table of being outdoors.

Our clients didn't want the kitchen to look like a traditional kitchen. They wanted the kitchen and dining to appear as one fluid space

THIS MODERNIST 1960S HOME overlooks Sydney Harbour, the bridge and the opera house. Given the spectacular outlook, it seemed inappropriate that the kitchen was cut off from this aspect. "The kitchen was seen as 'back of house'. There was no connection to the dining area," says architect Tony Chenchow, who removed the brick wall between the two rooms.

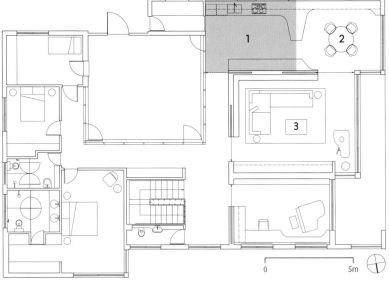

1 Kitchen
2 Dining room
3 Living room

The kitchen, located on the first floor of the house, was functional although slightly dated. With tiles on the floor and pokey cupboards, it didn't correspond to the quality of joinery in the rest of the house. "Our clients didn't want the kitchen to look like a traditional kitchen. They wanted the kitchen and dining to appear as one fluid space." **>>**

As well as removing a dividing wall, the design included new joinery and flooring. Cream rubber Pirelli floors were installed to complement the circular screen doors at the entrance to the house. Blackbean-timber veneer, used to clad the drawers in the kitchen, also relates to the blackbean-timber joinery used extensively in the living areas and bedrooms. To create a subtle division between the kitchen and dining areas, the architects cantilevered the timber joinery by approximately 1.2 metres.

To accentuate the ribbon of blackbean-joinery drawers, white polyurethane was used for the kitchen cupboards, both above and below the benches. A seamless effect was created by using white Corian for the splashbacks and benchtops, with a slight curvature joining the two planes. "The Corian was welded on-site to create the form," says Chenchow. Adding to the retro kitchen and dining area, copper pendant lights by Tom Dixon were included. "Our clients owned a Knoll table and chairs which fit in perfectly," says Chenchow, who extended the kitchen joinery into the dining area.

The architects retained the original sliding glass doors to the balcony. "You're not immediately aware that it's a new kitchen. It has that strong retro feel, while still being contemporary."

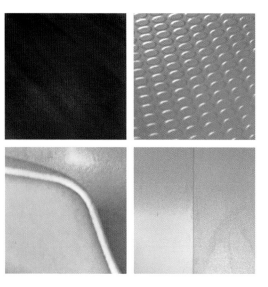

Our clients spend a lot of time in the kitchen so they didn't want to feel removed from what was going on

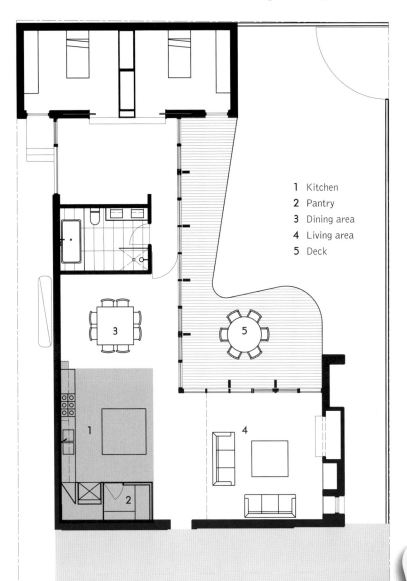

1 Kitchen
2 Pantry
3 Dining area
4 Living area
5 Deck

0   5m

ORIGINALLY BUILT IN THE 1930s, this house has been reworked by architect Clare Cousins. While the original rooms were retained in the renovation, the L-shaped 1950s addition was removed. "I'm respectful of modernist mid-century design, but this didn't fall into that category," says Cousins. Nevertheless, the shape of the 1950s addition was retained. "We're on a corner, so creating an L-shaped design maximised the light. It also took advantage of the plane trees in the street."

In contrast to the pitched roof of the original home, the new wing features generous glazing and an angular roofline. Unlike the smaller openings of the 1930s house, the addition includes floor-to-ceiling glass windows and doors. The roof is supported by fine steel columns to ensure the house could be opened up to the garden. "These were designed by our client (an engineer). The glass doors were designed to slide behind the (external) columns," says Cousins. A patio follows the line of the extension. >>

One of the owners works in a commercial kitchen so she knew what she wanted at home. A large island bench measuring 1.8 by 1.8 metres is a focal point of the kitchen. Made from stained Tasmanian oak with a concrete benchtop, the island bench includes cupboards, as well as shelves for cookbooks. "We wanted the bench to address the living areas, as much as the kitchen," says Cousins.

One of the other features of the kitchen is a walk-in pantry, clad in MDF and routed to appear as timber. Painted a charcoal-green hue, it appears as a distinctive form within the space. In contrast to the pantry, the kitchen cupboards below the sink are painted white. While there are cupboards above the bench in the kitchen, there are also open shelves made from stainless steel. "Our clients spend a lot of time in the kitchen so they didn't want to feel removed from what was going on, whether with the family or when entertaining friends," says Cousins.

The roof is punctured by four skylight openings that track the movement of the sun throughout the day

51

THIS PROJECT IS LOCATED opposite a small park and is within a heritage conservation area. The existing house is a single-storey Federation cottage. The clients are a family of five and the brief called for a four-bedroom house with an open-plan living/dining/kitchen area that needed to have a connection to outdoor entertaining and a new swimming pool.

The design solution was to extend to the rear and keep the existing house as a single-storey cottage, thereby providing a clear separation between the original house and the new extension. This separation is further enhanced by the relocated entry to the house. >>

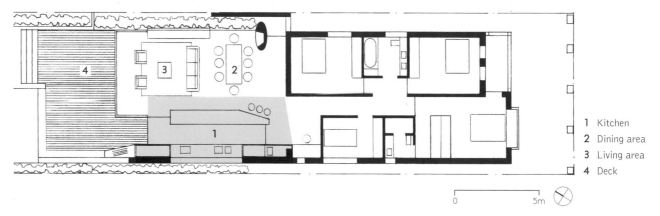

1 Kitchen
2 Dining area
3 Living area
4 Deck

0   5m

The new living/dining/kitchen area is defined by an off-form concrete roof supported by steel columns, which have been incorporated into the glazing system in order to make them disappear. The experience is that of a 'floating' concrete roof, which is further emphasised by the hanging wall to the east. The roof is punctured by four skylight openings that track the movement of the sun throughout the day. This open-plan space flows to an outdoor timber deck from which the pool is accessed via four steps. The roof floats past the glazed doors to create an overhang and provide sun control in summer to the north.

The kitchen runs the full length of the south-eastern wall. The overhead cupboards of the kitchen appear to float within the clear glass splashback and the highlight strip window running above them. The colour scheme of bubble-gum pink for the overhead cupboards and pale, willow green and off white were chosen to offset the industrial feel of grey concrete. The island bench anchors the entire space and is made of Corian. The splay of the island bench is a direct result of the circulation requirements of the space. The kitchen bench continues past the glass door to the outside deck to house the barbeque.

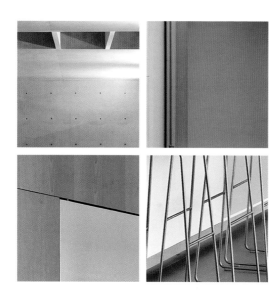

It's like a stage, where the performance of cooking takes place

THE OWNERS OF THIS house enjoy views over Sydney's Lane Cove River. However, this view isn't evident from the street. "It's only when you descend the stairs that the view opens up," says architect Vladimir Ivanov, co-director of Cullinan Ivanov Partnership.

The house, made from off-formed concrete, was designed for a couple with three children. "They wanted a house that was robust, averting anything that was showy," says Ivanov. The kitchen, located on the middle level, forms part of the open-plan living areas. On one side of the kitchen is the dining area, and on the other side is the lounge. All three areas lead to a terrace, with views of the river. The kitchen and dining area also have an aspect towards a feature sandstone wall and reflective pond. "We wanted to bring additional light into the kitchen and living areas," says Ivanov. **>>**

0   5m

1 Kitchen

2 Dining area

3 Living area

To define the kitchen from the living areas, the architects raised the kitchen one step. They also differentiated the kitchen from the living areas by using white rubber flooring in the kitchen, with charcoal stone tiles else-where. "It's like a stage, where the performance of cooking takes place," says Ivanov.

Central to the design of the kitchen is a 6-metre-long island bench. Made from white Corian, this bench cantilevers at one end to create a breakfast nook for the family. "We used Corian as we didn't want to see any seams in the surface," says Ivanov, who inserted a bright red polyurethane strip into the bench. Backlit, this strip glows at night.

Complementing the island bench is a wall of joinery, made from MDF, with a polyurethane finish in white. The architects used toughened glass as the splash-back, which reflects the sandstone wall. Light bouncing from the water in the reflective pond creates a magical effect.

"It's quite a simple kitchen. It's not over designed. The focus is on the water, as well as the ceiling (off-formed concrete). And on warmer days, there's nothing more pleasurable that eating breakfast on the terrace," says Ivanov.

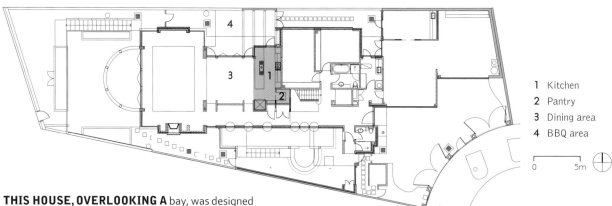

1 Kitchen
2 Pantry
3 Dining area
4 BBQ area

0   5m

THIS HOUSE, OVERLOOKING A bay, was designed for a couple scaling down from their family home. With adult children and grandchildren, the brief to Edgard Pirrotta & Associates was for a low-maintenance design that focused on the water views. "The kitchen and living areas (on the ground floor) are open plan. We wanted to frame views of the yachts, whether you were standing in the kitchen or sitting around the dining table," says architect Edgard Pirrotta.

The ground floor of the two-storey house features two guest bedrooms and bathrooms, together with the kitchen, dining and living areas. A terrace and courtyard wrap around the kitchen and living areas. "We wanted to make the living spaces as light and transparent as possible," says Pirrotta.

While the kitchen is open to the dining area, it is delineated by an island bench. Featuring a stone benchtop with two-pack-painted drawers and cupboards below, the design is pared back. To make access to drawers

We wanted to frame views of the yachts, whether you were standing in the kitchen or sitting around the dining table

and cupboards as easy as possible, large D-shaped handles appear on the joinery. The kitchen also features timber-veneer cupboards above the hotplates, as well as a Seraphic-glass splashback. "I generally don't like kitchen benches to be more than 1.5 metres apart. Everything should be at your fingertips," says Pirrotta, who included a walk-in pantry in the design. "The kitchen was designed for a couple rather than a family. The idea was to eliminate through traffic."

One of the pleasures of this kitchen is its connection to the outdoors. There's a courtyard adjacent to the kitchen, with its own separate door. From the dining area, as well as from the lounge, there are floor-to-ceiling sliding glass doors to the terrace. In the courtyard a copper pergola creates some protection from the elements. This protection is further increased by the overhang of the first floor where the main bedroom suite is located. To allow for alfresco dining, there's a built-in barbeque in the courtyard. "It acts as another room, particularly during the warmer months," he adds.

Our clients love to cook. But they also wanted to be included in conversations while they're preparing meals

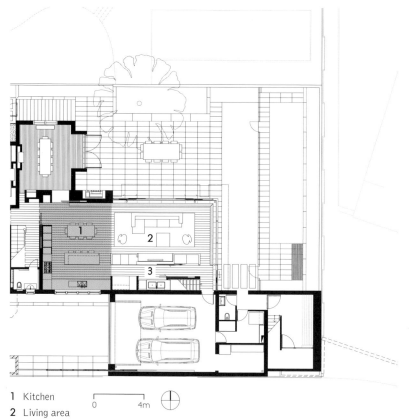

1 Kitchen
2 Living area
3 Laundry

0   4m

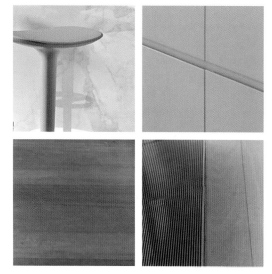

THIS LARGE 1920S HOME had more than enough rooms, but they weren't quite right for a family with adult children. "The rooms were fairly small and enclosed. There was little connection to the garden," says architect Franco Fiorentini, a co-director of F2 Architecture. "The house had been renovated in the 1980s, but still needed reworking."

One of the main shortfalls of the house was in the kitchen and informal living areas. A new open-plan area was added to the house, complete with floor-to-ceiling glass doors and glass walls. "We also added a second living area on the first floor for the grown-up children," says Fiorentini. **>>**

The new kitchen, located to one side of the open-plan living area, appears to have the original 1920s windows, however, these windows are an enlarged version of the original design. "We wanted to increase the amount of light into the kitchen," says Fiorentini. The kitchen is connected to a dining and informal-living area. "Our clients love to cook. But they also wanted to be included in conversations while they're preparing meals," he adds.

The kitchen features reconstituted stone benchtops, as well as extensive joinery made from MDF and painted in two-pack. Separating the kitchen from the living area is an island bench made from reconstituted stone and Calacatta marble (below the bench top). Used for informal meals, the island bench is also a good place to sit while catching up on the day's events.

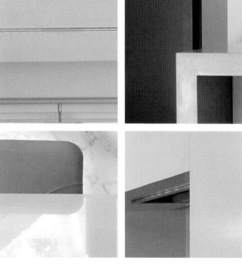

A walk-in pantry allows the kitchen to remain uncluttered. This area also contains a laundry as well as a staircase that leads to a living room at the top of the stairs. To ensure this area didn't appear claustrophobic, the architects created a gap between the top of the wall and the ceiling.

For F2 Architecture, designing a kitchen requires an understanding of how the owners prepare meals. "Each client has a unique way of cooking, and the kitchen must be tailor-made to them," adds Fiorentini.

Funnily enough, this kitchen is the exact opposite of what was originally requested

WHILE THIS 1930S HOUSE contained many period features, the kitchen and informal living areas were considerably more basic. The original kitchen was half the size it is now. Fortunately, the architect was able to incorporate space from an adjoining garage.

The design brief was quite succinct: The client prefers to have clean surfaces, with minimal clutter, so it was important to include generous storage. Initially the client preferred having the sink in the back corner of her kitchen so that dishes weren't the focal point of the design. Funnily enough, this kitchen is the exact opposite of what was originally requested. At the last minute, the client saw one of HP&G's darker, moodier kitchens. She loved that glamour, so the design ended up being the inverse of what was initially briefed (white joinery and dark benchtops).

The kitchen features reconstituted-stone benchtops and the joinery is quarter-cut timber-veneer in American oak, stained to match the American oak flooring. Graphic in feel, the kitchen is complemented by white Thonet bar stools. Even the pendant light follows the same black-and-white scheme. This colour scheme also strengthens the garden vistas, accentuated by the surrounding foliage.

While commandeering the space from the garage provided the initial solution, HP&G found the combined space almost too large. The solution was to include a utilities block that integrates the fridge, freezer and pantry, together with an office nook. Shutting these doors creates the impression of a timber-lined wall.

While previously the main view in the kitchen was towards a side fence, this kitchen looks directly over a rear courtyard, separated only by black-steel doors and windows. There's now a real connection from the kitchen to the pool, allowing direct sight lines to the children playing outside.

1 Kitchen
2 Dining area
3 Utilities block

0   5m

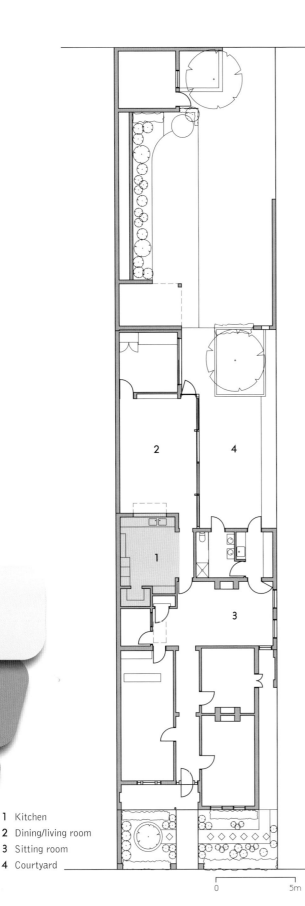

1 Kitchen
2 Dining/living room
3 Sitting room
4 Courtyard

0   5m

THE RENOVATION OF THIS Victorian house retained the original front rooms while adding new open-plan dining and living areas. Rather than demolish the original kitchen the architects retained it, simply opening it to a new living wing.

"We removed the original lean-to, including the windows. However, we wanted to integrate some of the original kitchen features in the design," says architect Jenny Rizzo, one of the directors of Inarc Architects, pointing out the original built-in timber dresser and open fireplace. "There's also a cellar below the pantry," she adds. These features have been painted white to appear integral to the new kitchen. The original timber floorboards have also been retained. "We wanted to create a traditional kitchen, but with a contemporary edge." >>

The original footprint of the kitchen remains intact, while new elements have been added

The original footprint of the kitchen remains intact, while new elements have been added. A large free-standing oven features on one side of the kitchen, nestled between the pantry and fireplace. To provide additional preparation space, the architects designed two steel-and-marble-top shelves either side of the oven.

The kitchen also includes a long marble bench, with open steel shelves below. A contemporary interpretation of a country-style kitchen, the shelves include open rattan baskets positioned on rails. "You can slide the baskets out to reach all your pots and pans, as well as plastic containers," says Rizzo. While there is a large opening between the kitchen and dining area, a marble splashback conceals any dirty dishes.

Like the kitchen, which blends new and old, meals are served around a period timber table with Alvar Aalto stools. "This is where the family tends to gather first thing in the morning. The dining area also tends to be the focal point at night," says Rizzo. And while the original house failed to connect to the garden, the architects created a courtyard garden adjacent to the new living wing. "Often, the family will dine outdoors during the warmer months."

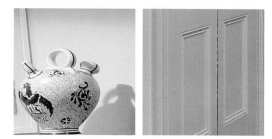

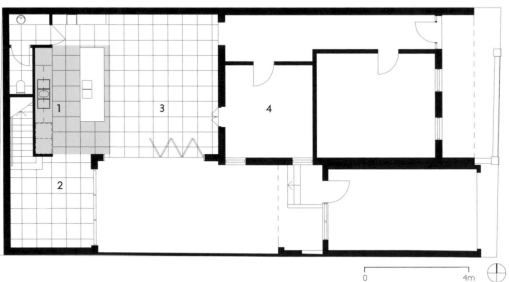

The doors to the powder room and the fridge are the only ones with handles

0   4m

1 Kitchen
2 Meals area
3 Family room
4 Dining room

71

THIS TWO-STOREY VICTORIAN terrace had been added to several times. "The additions were fairly erratic," says architect Robert Ficarra, one of three directors of Interlandi Mantesso Architects (IMA). The original parts of the home, including the formal lounge and dining area were retained in the latest renovation, as were the bedrooms on the first floor. However, the more recent additions, which included a kitchen, family room and laundry, were demolished. "We wanted to strengthen the connection to the courtyard, even if it is modest (3 by 7 metres)," says Ficarra.

Rather than replacing the additions with more enclosed rooms, IMA created one large open-plan kitchen and living area at the rear of the house. "Our client wanted one large space where she could relax as well as prepare meals," says Ficarra. The addition, which focuses on a side courtyard, is finished with stone flooring throughout. Central to the kitchen is an island bench, constructed in calacatta marble, with a mirrored front below. The green-tinged mirror increases the sense of space, as well as reflecting light. The architects also used the same type of mirror for the kitchen's splashbacks. **>>**

The kitchen joinery is a combination of two-pack painted cupboards, with extensive drawers, and cupboards made from timber veneer. A large timber-veneer cupboard adjacent to the stove appears like an extension of the kitchen itself, however, behind this door is a powder room. Also concealed are the fridge and freezer, located behind joinery doors on the other side of the kitchen. "The doors to the powder room and the fridge are the only ones with handles," says Ficarra, who was keen to create a minimal aesthetic.

As with many of the latest kitchens, IMA included a built-in coffee machine, and all the latest appliances, including a steamer.

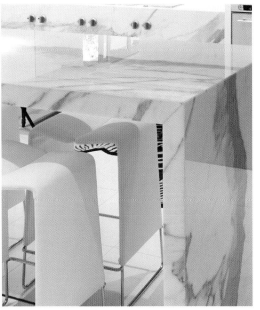

It's quite a grand family home, but not in the traditional sense

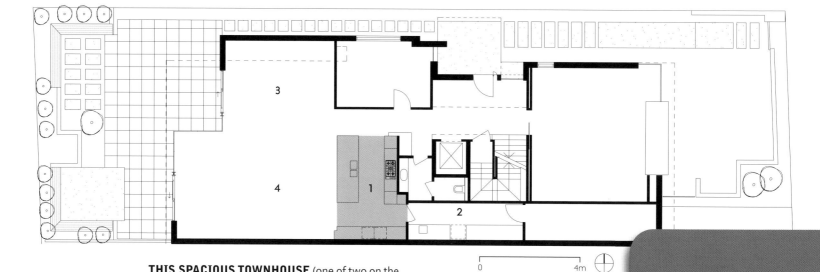

0   4m

1   Kitchen
2   Pantry
3   Meals area
4   Living area

THIS SPACIOUS TOWNHOUSE (one of two on the site) is spread over three levels. Measuring approximately 50 squares, this townhouse was designed for family living. "It's quite a grand family home, but not in the traditional sense," says architect Robert Ficarra, one of three directors of Interlandi Mantesso Architects (IMA).

The ground floor of the townhouse comprises the main living areas, including an open-plan kitchen, living and dining areas. These areas lead directly to a pool and landscaped terrace. "The garden is low maintenance, and there's more than enough room for outdoor dining," says Ficarra.

To create a sense of continuity, large porcelain tiles measuring 60 cm by 60 cm were used throughout the entire ground floor. To create a seamless effect between the kitchen and the living areas, the palette of materials is deliberately understated. The central island bench in the kitchen features a marble bench with white high-gloss MDF cupboards below. High-gloss cupboards, painted white, also feature in the kitchen joinery. "We tend to include large sliding drawers in our designs. They're ideal for large pots and pans," says Ficarra. **>>**

One wall of the kitchen includes a concealed fridge together with an exposed oven, coffee machine and microwave. To one side of the kitchen there is a telephone nook, together with a timber-veneer door that leads to a walk-in pantry. "It's quite a challenge making a kitchen integral to a living space," says Ficarra. "It has to be functional, yet you also want to be able to close it down when you're not using it."

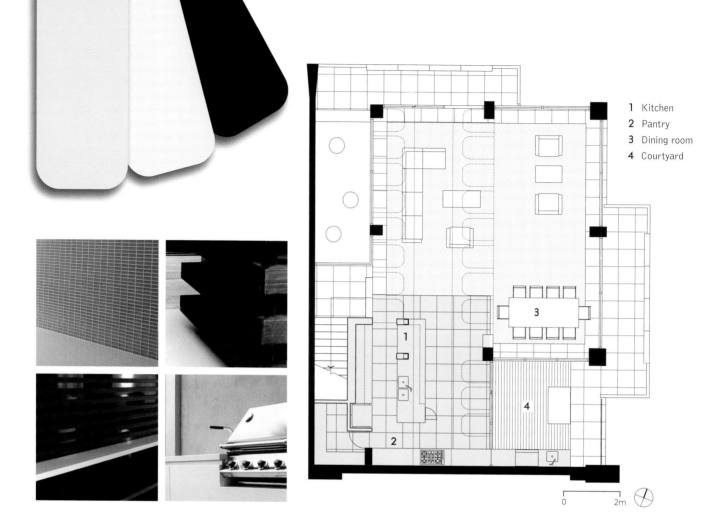

1 Kitchen
2 Pantry
3 Dining room
4 Courtyard

0   2m

We wanted to open up the kitchen to the living areas and terrace, as well as creating double-height spaces

THIS PENTHOUSE APARTMENT IN the city offered panoramic views, however, the view within was less impressive. "It was tired," says architect Zvi Belling, one of four directors of I.T.N. architects. While the architects 'touched' almost every room of this three level apartment, it was the kitchen and living areas that required the most attention. "We wanted to open up the kitchen to the living areas and terrace, as well as creating double-height spaces (in the living area)," says Belling.

While the plan to remove walls seemed relatively straightforward when looking at the original drawings, Belling quickly realised the presence of substantial structural columns. Rather than try to mask these, the two columns on the edge of the kitchen were highlighted. Clad in MDF, with a white two-pack painted finish, these columns are lined with high-gloss black laminate. As well as supporting the mezzanine, these columns now also double as display cases.

A dramatic element in the design is the kitchen's island bench. Made from black laminate (on the side of the living room) and clad with stained timber battens, the bench is framed by white reconstituted stone. The C-shaped surround also allows the owners to rest their feet on the lower shelf. To maximise storage, generous cupboards made from MDF were included on two sides of the kitchen. Lightboxes are concealed behind the cupboards above bench height. "We also recessed the lower cupboards and used a reflective laminate below," says Belling, who was keen to elevate the joinery above the black granite tiled floors. "This granite formed part of the original kitchen," he adds.

To engage with the city views, kitchen joinery was extended beyond the glass walls to the terrace. Designed as two pieces of joinery, two benches appear to pierce the glass wall, and to allow for alfresco dining, the outdoor joinery includes a built-in barbeque. The joinery on the terrace is made from Formboard, a wet-proof material used in ship building.

The kitchen and
informal-living areas
epitomise the ease
of living requested
by the owners

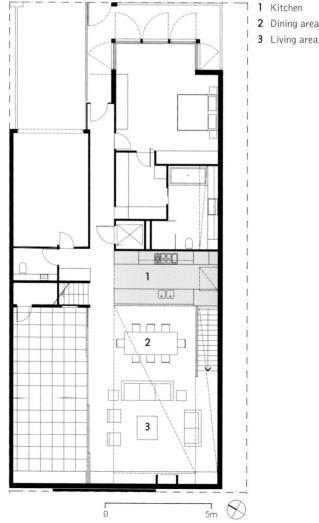

1 Kitchen
2 Dining area
3 Living area

THIS INNER-CITY HOUSE SITS on a compact site, approximately 9 metres wide by 30 metres deep. Constructed in stone, glass and zinc, the house was designed to complement the heritage streetscape. "Most of the period homes in the street are single fronted. We wanted to respect the rhythm of these homes," says architect Chris Manton, director of JAM Architects. "From a distance, our design could be interpreted as two houses joined together."

Designed for a couple who regularly travel, the brief was to create a low-maintenance home. The kitchen and informal-living areas, located on the ground floor at the rear of the house, epitomise the ease of living requested by the owners. At one end of the open-plan space is a galley-style kitchen, separated from the dining and living areas by an island bench. >>

0   5m

The kitchen, like the rest of the house, was designed in neutral tones and materials. The kitchen joinery, for example, features two-pack-painted joinery. For the splashback, as well as the island bench, Manton used reconstituted limestone. While the kitchen benches facing the living areas are kept free of clutter, there is a more concealed side of the kitchen devoted to food preparation, including a generous pantry. Like many kitchens, this one includes two separate sinks in the island bench. One of these sinks is used for rinsing dishes, while the other has a set of taps that provides filtered water and instant boiling water.

To create a seamless connection between the kitchen and living areas, the architects included limed ash on the ceiling, which extends to form a bank of cupboards in the living room. Two skylights were included, one on either side of the timber ceiling. "It's a fairly built up area. We wanted to maximise the light, while still preventing overlooking from neighbours," says Manton. Limed-ash shelves also appear in the island bench. On the dining side, these shelves provide a nook for objects or books.

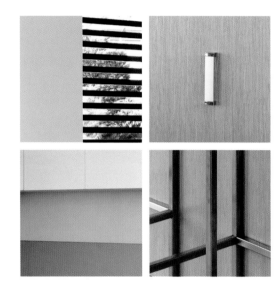

THE SITE FOR THIS family home was selected for its views overlooking the treed valley of the Moorabool River on the fringes of Geelong's Barrabool Hills. The challenge for Chris Manton, director of JAM Architects, was to design a contemporary, practical family home that captured these north-facing views while dealing with the extreme slope of the land. The client requested that ample outdoor living space and garden be maintained with direct access from the living areas. The result is a house structured over a series of levels, each addressing functional accommodation requirements internally, yet maintaining a direct connection to the external terraces of the garden.

Upon entering the first level from the central stair, the kitchen overlooks an open dining and living room arrangement that captures the spectacular views over the valley. This space connects directly with the outdoor entertaining area that overlooks the swimming pool on the upper terrace. Also on this level is the formal lounge room, with a large home office concealed behind with sliding doors to enable the spaces to interconnect. **>>**

The kitchen overlooks an open dining and living room arrangement that captures the spectacular views over the valley

1 Kitchen
2 Dining area
3 Living area

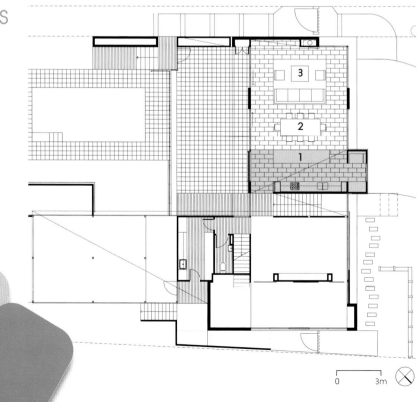

0 ___ 3m

The kitchen is centrally located and is the core of the home around which the family lives and entertains. The elongated rectangular plan allows for a large stone island bench around which family and friends gather. The island is designed to read as a freestanding piece of furniture, cantilevered over a stainless steel frame. To one end the underbench is kept open, forming a table and a full breakfast bar arrangement allowing for ample seating.

The rear bench accomodates the wash-up and cooking zones, removing the clutter of a functional kitchen from the island. The overhead cupboards, finished in two-pack, are framed by a portal of timber-veneered joinery, housing pantry units and ample storage.

Maintaining the open circulation, but to conceal the clutter of the family kitchen, a galley-type scullery is located at the eastern end of the kitchen. Timber battens to the window maintain a filtered natural light while ensuring privacy from the street.

1	Kitchen
2	Family area
3	Dining area

0   4m

My brief was to design a house around a central kitchen where the family could meet to have meals and find out about each other's day

THE OWNERS OF THIS house purchased the large site (with house) for its potential as a development site. The Edwardian style house had undergone a series of lean-to additions over a number of years and was not ideal for a family with four young sons. The owners decided to demolish the additions and extend the house to accommodate their needs in a contemporary but sympathetic style to the retained original part of the house. "My brief was to design a house around a central kitchen where the family could meet to have meals and find out about each other's day," says architect John Henry.

The laminate kitchen where this occurs forms an L-shape around a very large central island bench that can seat the six family members. It also forms part of the family room area that leads to a covered deck, and further beyond to the vast landscaped garden. The floor is made of recycled fire-damaged hardwood flooring that has been polished to accentuate the interesting pattern in the timber. The owners now hold each of the boys' birthday parties around the central bench where up to 30 schoolmates and relatives gather.

1   Kitchen
2   Dining area
3   Living area

THIS HOUSE WAS DESIGNED by its architect/owner John Henry for himself and his partner. The primary idea for the house was an open space where one area flows uninterrupted into another. Each area is located on a hovering platform that is supported above the natural ground, allowing the spaces underneath to flow into one another as well.

These areas form internal landscaped gardens that are viewed from the platforms. Some platforms have cantilevered extensions of clear Perspex floors that extend out over the gardens and an internal waterfall, allowing views to the areas immediately below. The platforms also have cascading plants that drop past other platforms and spaces.

The whole space is covered by a large kit farm shed with a translucent roof that allows light to reach the indoor garden plants. The rear wall of the shed is clear glass and looks out over a leafy gully. The linear kitchen is located at one end of the entry/dining area and is screened from the main dining area by a mobile bench unit with hob.

"This unit is the informal hub area where meals are served. It also acts as an area where guests can gather to indulge in conversation, pre-dinner snacks and drinks. That allows the person in the kitchen to be part of the conversation and not feel left out" says Henry. The kitchen area also flows through double doors to the outside barbeque and eating area.

The primary idea for the house was an open space where one area flows uninterrupted into another

Time and motion are fundamental when designing a kitchen

WHEN THE OWNERS, a young couple with a child, bought this 1930s house it was in almost original condition with only a few changes having been made over the years. "The only things we had to remove were a laundry and toilet. We converted the original kitchen into a bathroom," says architect John Henry.

Henry designed a large two-storey addition, comprising an open-plan kitchen, dining and living areas on the ground floor. On the first floor are the main bedroom, ensuite and second bedroom. As there is a slight fall in the land, Henry created a change in level between the informal living and dining areas. Access to the new wing from the lower level is via a corridor and across a glazed bridge-like structure. **>>**

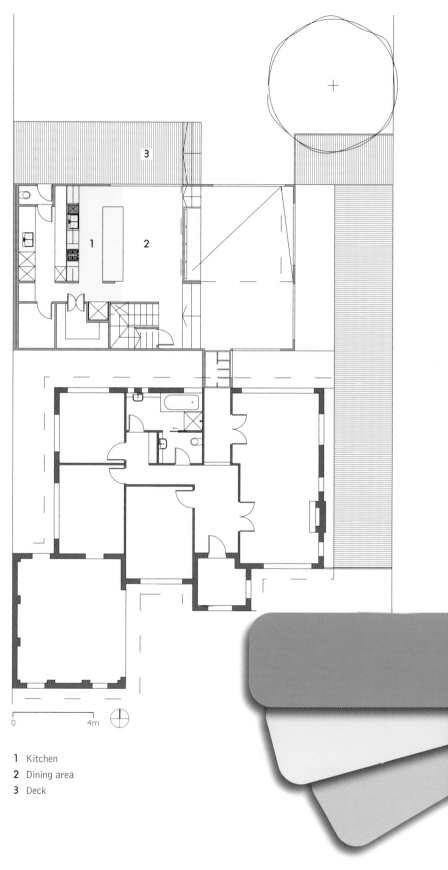

0   4m

1 Kitchen
2 Dining area
3 Deck

Like the dining and living areas, the new kitchen features polished concrete floors and enjoys framed garden views through glass sliding doors to the terrace. "The timber decks (external) are an extension of the kitchen," says Henry. Rather than compete with the garden aspect, Henry designed a minimal and sleek kitchen. Featuring extensive joinery made from a putty-coloured laminate, the kitchen includes extensive cupboard space, both above and below the reconstituted-stone benches. One of the few appliances on display is the large oven.

According to Henry, 'time and motion' are fundamental when designing a kitchen. "The triangular-shaped arrangement still holds," he says, pointing out the location of the stove, sink and bench. "Kitchens have to be efficient, as well as being pleasurable spaces to work in."

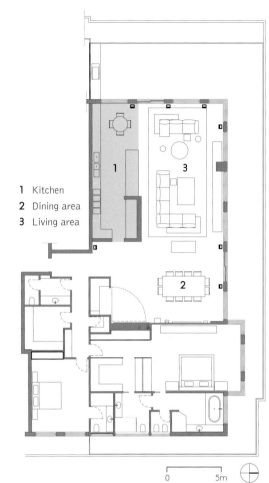

1 Kitchen
2 Dining area
3 Living area

0   5m

I didn't want the kitchen to impede on my client's collection of art

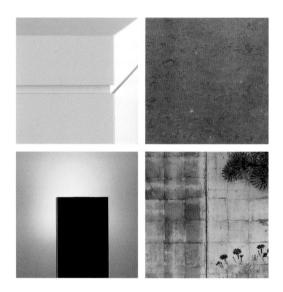

THIS PENTHOUSE APARTMENT HAS spectacular city views. Although the original fitout was relatively new, its palette of materials was quite dark. "The walls were timber panelled. The apartment seemed quite oppressive. And it wasn't an ideal arrangement for my client's art collection," says architect Stephen Jolson.

Jolson gutted the penthouse apartment, removing the heavy timber panels, creating a considerably lighter palette. Stone floors feature in the kitchen, and instead of timber cupboards there are white Corian benches and two-pack painted cupboards in the same colour as the benchtops. "They read like pieces of furniture," says Jolson, who also used Corian for the splashbacks in the kitchen. And to draw one's eye to the city views, Jolson extended the kitchen bench beyond the glass sliding doors to the terrace. **>>**

Apart from the rangehood, there are no kitchen cupboards above the benches. Many of the appliances, as well as a fridge and pantry, are tucked away to one side of the kitchen, concealed by two-pack painted joinery. As the owners love to cook, there is a sophisticated range of appliances in the kitchen, including a steamer and a wok. "I've used a simple palette of materials. I didn't want the kitchen to impede on my client's collection of art," pieces of which have been collected over many years says Jolson.

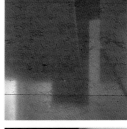

A distinctive feature of the kitchen is the sliding wall that separates the kitchen and meals area from the living room. "You can easily slide the wall across and close the kitchen entirely," says Jolson. Although the meals area is bathed in light for most of the day, the owners regularly dine on the terrace that wraps around the apartment on three sides. "Previously, there was a galley-style kitchen. There was almost no connection to the outdoors," he adds.

1	Kitchen	
2	Lounge/dining area	
3	Covered entertaining area	

0   5m

My clients wanted a much larger house, but they didn't want a high-maintenance design

THIS SITE WAS ORIGINALLY occupied by a single-level house that was designed in the 1960s. While the owners appreciated the light-filled aspect and generous glazing, the house was too small, with minimal off-street car parking (the new garage holds up to seven cars). "My clients wanted a much larger house, but they didn't want a high-maintenance design," says architect Stephen Jolson.

The kitchen, located on the first floor, is the first room at the top of the entry staircase. Beautifully proportioned, the separate kitchen and open-plan living and dining areas lead to a large terrace with a gas bonfire. This creates a focal point for alfresco dining, as well as providing an outdoor room during the cooler months.

The kitchen features a travertine island bench, 1.1 metres wide by 3.5 metres long, that is framed by wall-to-wall two-pack-joinery. The only feature of the island bench is the taps. "I wanted to use a limited palette of materials. The travertine is easy to maintain and it has a lovely horizontal grain," says Jolson, who also used travertine on the floors. **>>**

On one side of the kitchen is a wall of cupboards, two-pack finished, that conceal a pantry and a storage area. One of the cupboards features a slide-out appliance tray for the toaster and kettle. One notable feature of Jolson's design is the absence of overhead cupboards. "You need to think how the kitchen is going to be used. It's awkward for people to reach high cupboards," says Jolson.

One other distinguishing feature of the kitchen is the length of the bench, which extends to the terrace through glass sliding doors. The joinery on the terrace includes a built-in barbeque as well as additional storage. "This bench is approximately 10 metres long. I wanted to also extend the sight lines towards the city views," says Jolson.

To allow the owners to use the terrace throughout the year, Jolson designed a bronze canopy immediately outside the kitchen. With a built-in heater in the canopy, the owners can dine on the terrace well into the cooler months.

The generous kitchen and living area lead to a garden terrace, concealed behind the original factory walls

THIS BUILDING WAS ORIGINALLY a confectionary factory. While the building's orange brick walls and steel-framed windows hark back to the 1950s, the interiors are sleek and contemporary. Now a home and office for architect Stephen Jolson, the two uses are completely separated. Jolson's office is located on the ground floor, and the two-storey house above is accessed by a dramatic folded steel staircase.

An open-plan kitchen, dining and living areas, together with a bathroom and play area for Jolson's son, extend across the first floor. Approximately 22 metres wide by 10 metres deep, the generous kitchen and living area lead to a garden terrace, concealed behind the original factory walls.

Jolson conceived the spatial planning of the kitchen and living areas as three blocks. The first of these blocks, made from stained American oak, conceals the steel staircase. The doors, which fold back, conceal a bar lined with glass shelving for use in the dining area, an appliance cupboard, a fridge, a freezer and an oven. To one side of this wall of cupboards is a walk-in pantry.

The second block in the kitchen is concealed behind an operable canvas screen, 6 metres wide by 3.5 metres high, that slides across a track. "I wanted to create flexible spaces. It can function as a kitchen," says Jolson, sliding the screen to reveal cooktops and kitchen appliances. Moving the screen in the other direction exposes a home study. Jolson was also keen to expose some of the building's history. "When I bought the building, I was handed a magazine from 1955. Inside was a small photo showing a man standing at a large vat making sweets." Jolson enlarged the image and transposed it onto a canvas screen.

The third block in the living areas is the wall containing the fireplace. This wall separates the kitchen and lounge from the play area.

One of the most dramatic features in the kitchen is a 6-metre-long island bench. Made from black granite, the reflective monolith includes a double sink. "It's the only reflective surface in the kitchen. Everything else is matte-finished," says Jolson.

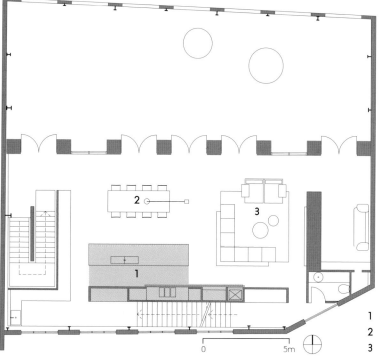

1   Kitchen

2   Dining area

3   Lounge

Glass doors can be
pulled back to create
an unimpeded space
between the inside
and the outside

110

111

THIS RENOVATION WAS INSPIRED by a grand
piano. The client, a pianist, spends endless hours practising. Architect Patrick Kennedy, a co-director of the
practice, also has an appreciation for the sound and
form of the piano. "The form lends itself to long narrow
sites, particularly when privacy from neighbours is
required," says Kennedy.

The piano is located in the formal sitting area at the
front of the house. The front sitting room, as well as bedrooms, feature felt-green coloured walls and ceilings.
The form of the piano is also expressed in the new
wing. A sculptural wall made from vertical timber and
painted in high-gloss black leads to the kitchen and
meals area. This wall is also a functional element,
concealing a bathroom/powder room and a separate
laundry. Behind this wall is a void, allowing natural
light to filter into the bathroom. **>>**

1 Kitchen
2 Meals
3 Living
4 Outdoor living

0   5m

The curvaceous wall includes an appliance cupboard and pantry as part of the kitchen. An integrated fridge is included in the design. In the centre of the kitchen is a steel-framed island bench with a laminated-timber bench top. Open-timber slatted shelves give the unit an industrial aesthetic. "Our clients didn't want a 'slick' kitchen," says architect Rachel Nolan. This is also expressed in the steel unit above the island bench. Used to hang pots and pans, as well as frame the hanging light bulbs, this unit is both functional and aesthetic.

And like the felt-green colour used in other parts of the house, the kitchen ceiling is also green. "Silver birch trees in the garden further 'green' the house," says Nolan, who appreciates the dappled light coming into the kitchen through the wall of trees. "The sun animates the kitchen in the afternoon," she adds.

The architects were keen to strengthen the connection between the kitchen and garden. Glass doors can be pulled back to create an unimpeded space between the inside and the outside. And to maximise the use of the courtyard-style garden, the architects included a covered patio to the rear of the home. Made from steel (painted black) and glass, this patio allows the garden to be used for a considerable part of the year.

ORIGINALLY BUILT IN THE 1930s, this stockbroker-tudor style house required considerable reworking to create a family home. "It was a large house. But it was a warren of rooms, and the rooms were unfairly distributed," says architect Rachel Nolan, a co-director of Kennedy Nolan Architects. "The children's bedrooms were tucked into the roof space," she adds.

One of the areas that required most attention was the kitchen. Tacked onto the back of the house, this kitchen turned its back on to the garden. "We wanted to open up the kitchen, while still making it feel integral to the original home," says Nolan.

The architect created a pavilion linking the living areas at the front of the house to the kitchen and informal-living areas. The pavilion features leadlight windows that are sympathetic to the style of the original home. The kitchen, which leads from the pavilion, cleverly fuses the past with the present. Along one side of the kitchen, for example, is a wall of timber panelling that conceals a pantry, a fridge, and a storage area as well as a secret door to the main bedroom.

The kitchen also features an island bench, primarily designed for food preparation, which has a Corian benchtop with tapered steel legs. It is also used as extra bench space, a breakfast table, and informal meals area. The kitchen joinery highlights the architects' ability to fuse the past with the present. The factory-painted finished cupboards, for example, include a steel rail below the ceiling that allows a ladder to access the higher cupboards. While one part of the kitchen is visible from the living areas, part of the kitchen joinery is recessive. "This part of the kitchen is more like the butler's kitchen. It's where most of the food preparation occurs," says Nolan.

The owners now have an unimpeded view of the garden and swimming pool from the kitchen. Part of the renovation also included opening up the formal dining area to the kitchen. "People rarely eat formally. The dining room now feels part of the kitchen," adds Nolan.

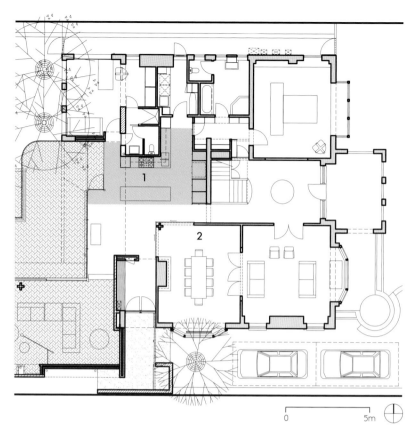

0   5m

1 Kitchen
2 Dining room

It was a warren of rooms, and the rooms were unfairly distributed

1 Kitchen
2 Living/dining
3 Courtyard

0   5m

For inspiration they looked to the simple beach houses of the 1950s and 60s

WHEN ARCHITECTS ANNABEL LAHZ and her partner Andrew Nimmo designed their dream home at Casuarina Beach, on the northern coast of New South Wales, they were on a tight budget, so for inspiration they looked to the simple beach houses of the 1950s and 60s. Like many homes from this period, the Casuarina Beach house is constructed of face blockwork and fibre-cement sheets. Timber screening adds warmth and texture to the design. "The house also had to be functional for our two children and two dogs," says Lahz.

The kitchen, located on the ground floor of the two-storey house, focuses on an internal courtyard. "We saw the kitchen as the 'cockpit'. It's pivotal to holidays," says Lahz, referring to the series of meals prepared during the day. "We also wanted it to connect to the courtyard, which functions as an outdoor room during the warmer weather." **>>**

Like the style popular in the 1950s, the kitchen features exposed concrete-block walls and painted concrete floors. "It's an area that gets considerable traffic. We wanted something that was both serviceable and inexpensive," says Lahz. The kitchen features an island bench with a reconstituted-stone benchtop. This bench includes bright-yellow laminate on one side, and deep drawers and open shelves for crockery on the other. The drawers, approximately 350 millimetres deep, are ideal for storing large pots and pans. Although there is a pantry, it is relatively modest in size. "There's less cupboard space here than in many suburban homes. But when we come down, we only buy enough groceries for the week," says Lahz.

118

119

Connecting the kitchen to the living area was also important. A few steps above the kitchen, the living and dining areas are integrated in the space. And while the family enjoys sharing a meal around the dining-room table, they also appreciate the experience of dining in the courtyard. Although the courtyard is open to the sky, there is a partially covered courtyard on the other side of the living area for inclement weather. "When you're on holidays, it's about connecting to the outdoors," says Lahz, who included sliding glass doors between the kitchen and courtyard.

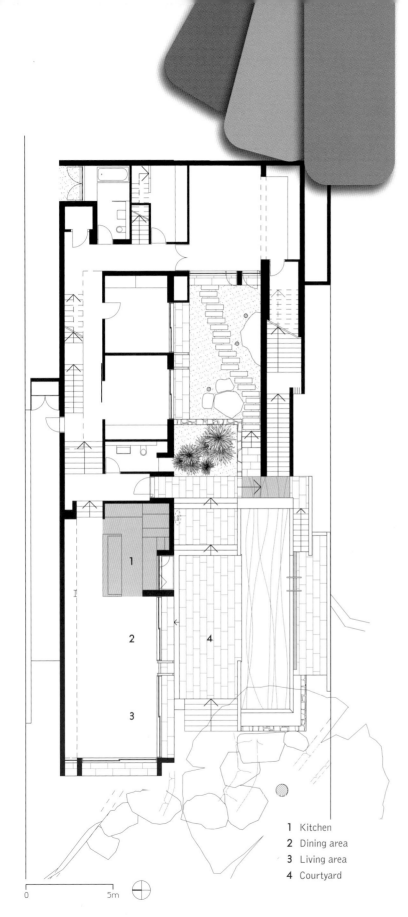

120
121

1 Kitchen
2 Dining area
3 Living area
4 Courtyard

0   5m

While the kitchen is open to the dining area, the structural supports, including a steel column and concrete pillar, provide a level of demarcation

AS THIS SITE HAS a sharp gradient, the house, designed by architect Louise Nettleton, is spread over three levels. The trajectory to the kitchen, located at ground level, appears at the end of a ribbon-like timber staircase. While the treads are numerous, the descent rewards with a view of Sydney Harbour, complete with bobbing yachts on the water's edge.

The kitchen, linked to the open-plan dining and living areas, also provides access to the terrace and lap pool. Large sliding glass doors frame the dining and living areas. In the kitchen, directly above the oven and hot-plates, there is a fold-out window. "Our clients didn't want us to include a rangehood. They prefer a continual flow of fresh air," says Nettleton. **>>**

While the kitchen is open to the dining area, the structural supports, including a steel column and concrete pillar, provide a level of demarcation. To complement the extensive use of concrete, both in the structural columns and ceiling, the architect used an American cherry wood for the kitchen joinery. On one side of the kitchen there are two sets of built-in cupboards that contain stereo equipment, and on the other side, adjacent to the island bench, there are two fridges and a freezer also concealed behind joinery, and delineated by the vents in the timber.

As the owners wanted a streamlined kitchen, a large walk-in pantry has been included, immediately adjacent to the hotplates. This pantry not only provides storage for food, but also includes a second dishwasher, as well as a second sink for preparation. "You're not really aware there's this much space behind the door," says Nettleton. A sculptural island bench in the centre of the space, made from Corian with stainless-steel benchtops, appears more like a piece of furniture separating the working part of the kitchen from the main thoroughfare.

Although the kitchen enjoys light-filled views of the harbour, Nettleton included a narrow skylight to one side of the kitchen that extends into the dining and living areas.

122

123

THIS NEW TWO-STOREY house enjoys a unique aspect over parkland and the city skyline. "The house is fairly closed from the street, but opens up the further you proceed," says architect Luigi Rosselli. The kitchen and living areas are located at the rear of the house, where the views and light are optimised. "Our client was quite specific in his brief. He wanted a kitchen that also accommodated two cats," says Rosselli, who included a basement space below the kitchen for the pets. Accessed from an opening in the wall, the 'cat house' includes a set of brick stairs and lighting activated by movement. "But you will generally find the cats on the deck," he adds.

A galley-style kitchen is located at the end of a curvaceous spine wall. Designed to display photographs and small objects, this wall creates a link to the living room, as well as the kitchen. Like the house, the kitchen is minimal and pared back. Reconstituted stone benches complement the two-pack MDF joinery. To create a streamlined effect, the kitchen splashbacks are made of glass. "The only free-standing unit in the kitchen is the oven," says Rosselli.

Most of the preparation is carried out in the area adjacent to the pantry. Complete with a second sink, it allows the main bench space to remain free of dishes and food. "It's a relatively simple design. But it suits our client's needs," says Rosselli. To add a splash of colour in the otherwise monochromatic scheme, a bank of 'pop-out' cupboards were included. Finished in a ribbed glass, these cupboards provide valuable storage space.

Our client was quite specific in his brief. He wanted a kitchen that also accommodated two cats

The deck also forms an important part of the kitchen, particularly during the warmer months. Glass stackable doors open onto the deck and are designed to pull back completely, or one door at a time. To ensure sun protection, there is a retractable blind on the inside, together with an automated awning below the eave. "When you're on the deck, you feel as though you're suspended well above the ground," says Rosselli, referring to the rock face below.

124
125

1 Kitchen
2 Pantry
3 Dining area
4 Living area

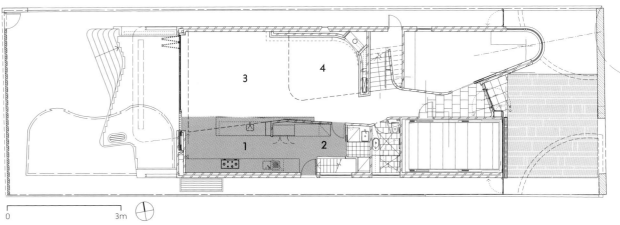

0   3m

FOR THE OWNERS OF this house, builder Dean Atkinson and his wife Dana, the elevated bayside site provided an ideal location to create a family home. "There was a fairly ordinary 1950s timber home on the site. It didn't take advantage of the site or the views," says Dean.

The brief to Maddison Architects was to design a contemporary home using low-maintenance materials, and to avoid paint-rendered walls. "I also wanted the house to express the materials for what they are, rather than create a veil," says architect Peter Maddison, referring to the black zinc that wraps around the kitchen and living wing in the house.

Pushing out the 'black box' to the street was an attempt to maximise views of the bay, as well as capture additional light. The zinc box not only makes its presence felt in the street, but is also slightly off-centre. The zinc panels are arranged at 15 degrees and appear on the 'underbelly' of the kitchen and informal living areas. The open-plan kitchen and living areas, located on the first floor, lead to an outdoor terrace. To ensure this terrace is used throughout the year it includes a cut-out ceiling with automated steel shutters. "We wanted a fairly casual home, nothing that felt stitched up," says Dean, who built the house. The terrace can also be accessed from the main bedroom. **>>**

We wanted a fairly casual home, nothing that felt stitched up

126

127

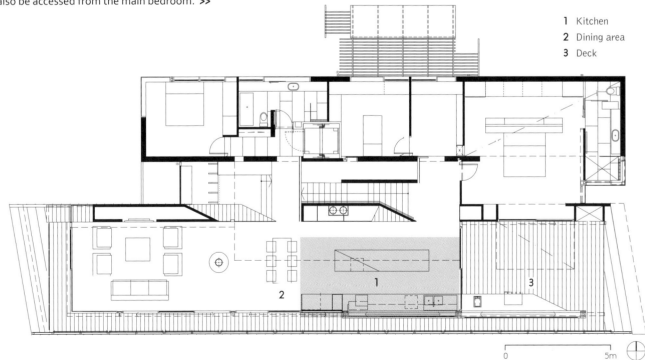

1 Kitchen
2 Dining area
3 Deck

0   5m

The kitchen, which acts as the hub of the house, features a long stone bench that is ideal for sitting around as well as for preparing food. To ensure the cook can enjoy water views, the sink and hotplates are positioned below an elongated picture window. A bank of timber cupboards on one side of the kitchen conceals most of the appliances, as well as providing storage. And with children, both Maddison and the Atkinsons were mindful of acoustic control, so sisal was applied to the angled ceiling to reduce the sound of footsteps on the timber floors.

There is also a second kitchen at ground level. Protected by the first floor, it's ideally located between the children's rumpus room and the swimming pool.

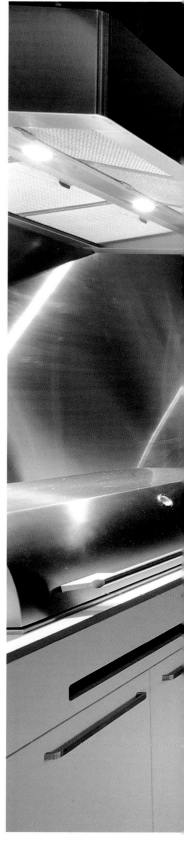

It was important to create a number of comfortable spaces

ARCHITECT MARCUS O'REILLY installed a new kitchen when renovating his own home. The original kitchen, tacked onto the back of his Edwardian house, formed part of a series of ad hoc additions. "There were a series of skillion roofs, each one getting lower as you moved towards the rear garden," says O'Reilly.

O'Reilly removed the additions, including the kitchen, a living area and a bedroom, and added a contemporary two-storey addition. Made from rendered brick, zinc-alume and plywood, the new wing features an open-plan kitchen, dining and living area at ground level, together with a main bedroom suite on the first floor.

"It's quite a large space. It was important to create a number of comfortable spaces," says O'Reilly. There's a small sitting nook that leads from the corridor, and the living area is slightly enclosed with a box-bay window seat. "The sight lines are open, but the spaces are defined," he adds. >>

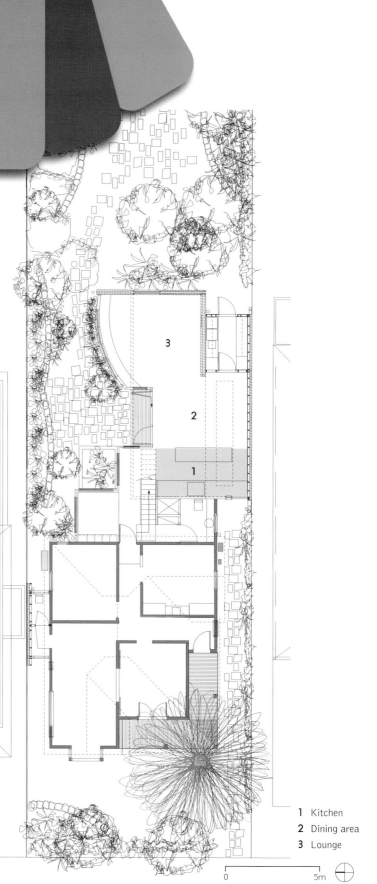

1 Kitchen
2 Dining area
3 Lounge

0   5m

The kitchen, located at one end of the living areas, features an island bench made from American oak and a white stone benchtop. The bench includes large drawers as well as cupboards for appliances. And to create a sense of lightness, the bench is slightly elevated above the timber floors on stainless-steel legs. "I wanted the kitchen to feel integral to the living areas," says O'Reilly, pointing out the alpine-ash floors used throughout.

The kitchen also includes rock-maple cupboards to conceal a fridge and pantry as well as white-textured laminate cupboards. For additional light, a glazed roof light has been inserted in the coffered ceiling. Previously, the kitchen turned its back on the garden, but the new kitchen features large sliding doors to a side garden. To maximise the garden's use during the warmer months there is a moveable outdoor table, together with built-in stone benches, the colour of which picks up some of the hues in the kitchen joinery.

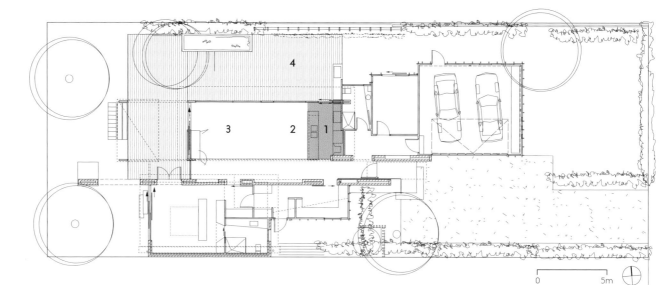

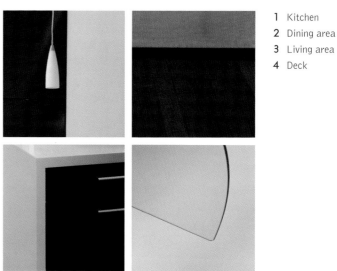

1 Kitchen
2 Dining area
3 Living area
4 Deck

A central spine between the two roofs splits the house into public and private functions

WHILE APPROPRIATELY SCALED FOR the neighbourhood this single-story house is a variation on the local typology. Whereas the typical suburban model of a distinct front and back yard is the norm in the area, this design focuses the house to a generous north-facing outdoor room. Stretching east to west across the site, the dynamic double-skillion roofs provide ample northern light into every room in the house. A central spine between the two roofs splits the house into public and private functions and visually connects the entrance to the sculptural forms of the rear garden. A thickened wall with deep niches for the display of art and random artifacts heightens the experience of passing along the central circulation. **>>**

The client, furniture-maker David Emery, and architect Marcus O'Reilly once shared a furniture workshop and over the years the pair have collaborated extensively. The longstanding working relationship between the two led to a very smooth, efficient and effective construction process, where both client and architect were consistently in agreement. The client's ease in understanding the design intent left time to focus on more intimate detailing such as the fine tapering of the roof eaves, the pocketing doors, and exterior cladding systems. The client brought his cabinet-making sensibility to the intricately coordinated construction of the house.

The kitchen design uses a simple galley arrangement, with the space extending to the outside deck, giving close access to the barbeque. The concealed pantry is spacious and is easily accessed and loaded up from the island bench, keeping the workflow very efficient.

The fridge is behind doors to keep the whole appearance simple and elegant, which is an important consideration in this particularly simple uncluttered open-plan environment.

The front panel is made of polished concrete. This slab has the hot-water pipes for the hydronic-heating system running through it, so that like all the hydronic-heating panels in this open-plan area they are integrated into the building fabric and thus hidden from view.

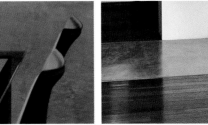

APART FROM THE TWO front rooms, which were restored, the remainder of this house is almost new, including a two-storey addition to the rear. "We wanted to maintain the heritage streetscape. The two front rooms were also in relatively good condition," says interior designer Debbie Ryan, of McBride Charles Ryan.

The kitchen, towards the rear of the house, sits between an informal dining area at one end and an informal living area at the other. Framed by the rear garden and an outdoor deck to one side, the indoor and outdoor spaces are blurred. "In the warmer weather, the doors are pulled back, with the curtain activating the spaces," says Ryan. **>>**

138

139

Framed by the rear garden and an outdoor deck to one side, the indoor and outdoor spaces are blurred

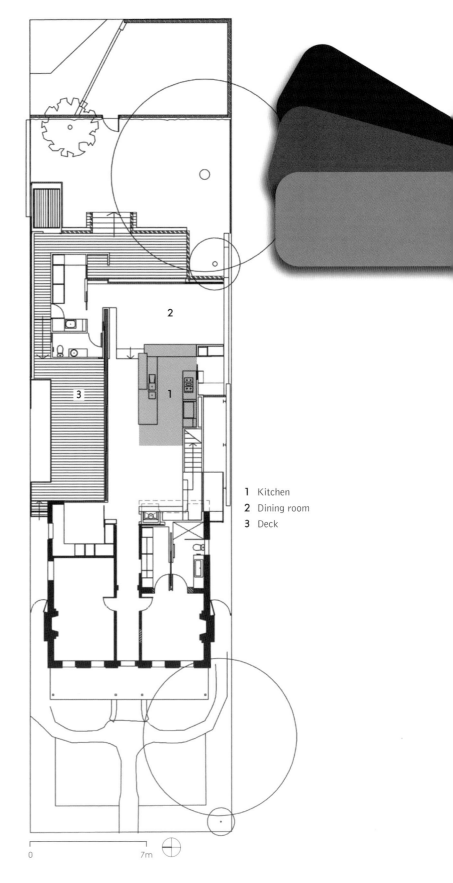

1 Kitchen
2 Dining room
3 Deck

0   7m

The L-shaped kitchen features an island bench, made from Corian and reconstituted stone. This bench wraps around the kitchen on two sides, providing additional preparation space, as well as separation from the dining area a few steps below. To ensure dirty dishes aren't noticeable from the dining table, MCR included a 'pop-out' in the bench. Additional joinery clad in Corian functions as an appliance cupboard.

To complement the Corian, a fiddleback-ash veneer was used for the kitchen cupboards. Even the fridge has been clad in veneer, allowing it to appear recessive in the open-plan space. To unify the kitchen and living areas, timber floorboards appear throughout.

"The design of the kitchen was centred on the garden. Whether you're sitting around the dining table, or sitting around the bench in the kitchen, you're connected to the outdoors," says Ryan.

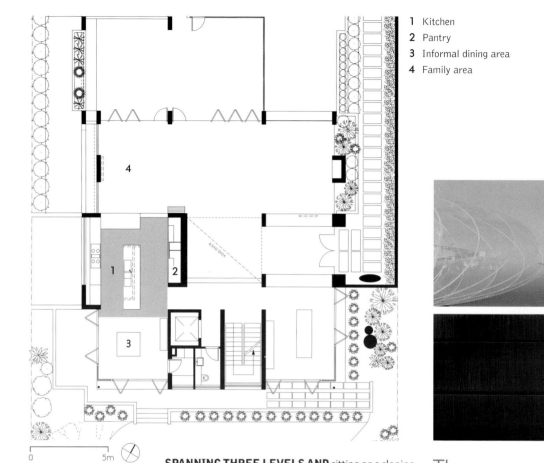

1 Kitchen
2 Pantry
3 Informal dining area
4 Family area

0   5m

SPANNING THREE LEVELS AND sitting on a sloping site, this house is monumental. "Our clients were looking for a large site where they could build a substantial home that was relatively private," says architect Tony Freeman, co-director of Molnar Freeman Architects.

Freeman, who works with his life and business partner, architect Katie Molnar, was partially inspired by the 1960s homes found in the Los Angeles hills. "Our clients are also taken by post-war architecture," says Freeman. As well as the clean and minimal lines of the period, the owners wanted large spaces to entertain friends and family. "They requested a variety of spaces to entertain, both indoor and outdoor," he adds. **>>**

The owners wanted large spaces to entertain friends and family

To create privacy from the street, the house is located near the rear of the property. The swimming pool, located at the front of the house, acts as a buffer. Loggias, adjacent to the pool, form another protective layer. "We wanted to create a variety of spaces for entertaining," says Freeman, who included an outdoor kitchen adjacent to the pool.

The main kitchen is located towards the rear of the home. Framed by stackable glass doors, the kitchen and informal-meals area lead to a terrace, with the garden a few steps above it. Central to the kitchen is a large island bench featuring a cantilevered polished-concrete benchtop that is an ideal place for family and friends to gather.

In keeping with the clean and minimal lines of the house, the architects used a limited palette of materials in the kitchen. Polyurethane cupboards feature extensively and conceal a fridge. The lower joinery, with extensive drawers, is predominantly made from timber veneer. Unifying the two materials are Corian benchtops, as well as a splashback and built-in shelf, also made from Corian. "It's a fairly neutral colour scheme," says Freeman, pointing out the large white tiles on the floor. "Most of the colour comes from the garden."

THIS ARTS-AND-CRAFTS-STYLE (circa 1914) home had been renovated in the 1990s. But even though the fit-out was functional, the addition didn't connect to the period home, or the garden. "The ceiling in the kitchen and informal living areas was extremely low, and the brick walls almost eliminated garden views," says interior designer Sioux Clark, co-director of Multiplicity, who worked closely on this project with her partner, architect Tim O'Sullivan.

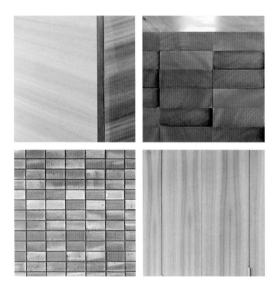

The materials used in the kitchen are slightly raw and soft

146

147

While the terracotta-tiled roof was retained in the new wing, the brick walls were removed and replaced with fine black steel columns. "We saw these columns like tree trunks in a forest," says O'Sullivan. Integral to the connection with the outdoors was the inclusion of sliding steel-and-glass doors, together with raising the existing timber deck. "Previously, you would have to step down to the garden. Now, the deck acts as an extension of the kitchen and living areas." >>

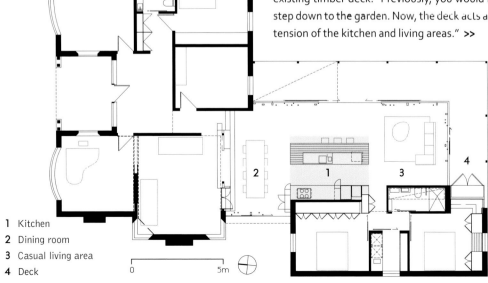

1 Kitchen
2 Dining room
3 Casual living area
4 Deck

0   5m

The brief was to strengthen the connection to the landscape and increase the natural light. The owners didn't want a minimal kitchen with hard reflective surfaces. As a consequence, the materials used in the kitchen are slightly raw and soft. Recycled spotted gum on the floor is oiled rather than finished with high gloss. The 4-metre-long island bench also features feathered timber edges rather than sharp lines. O'Sullivan was driving behind a truck and noticed the way timber had been roughly stacked. "All the edges jutted out," he recalls.

The island bench is finished with matte-glazed green tiles, flecked with copper. "The tiles have a slightly 1970s retro feel to them," says Clark, who used stainless steel for the benchtop. The joinery behind the island bench is also a combination of materials. Spotted-gum veneer was used for the overhead kitchen cupboards. The cupboards below the Corian bench have a two-pack-paint finish. Both these cupboards and the ceiling are in the same dark green-black hue. "At first, there was concern that it would be cave-like. But it accentuates the garden," says Clark.

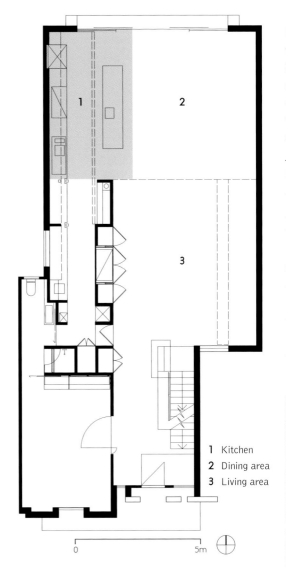

1 Kitchen
2 Dining area
3 Living area

0   5m

REWORKING SOMEONE ELSE'S design can be difficult. In this case Multiplicity was asked to rework a house that was designed by another practice. "We made minor changes to the exterior, as well as reworking most of the interior spaces," says architect Tim O'Sullivan, who realised from the start that the original design fell short of meeting the needs of these clients. "It wasn't just the nature of the spaces. The fit-out as was proposed was functional, but fairly generic."

While the original footprint of the building wasn't altered dramatically, the interior was customised for the family. Past the front door are a study and powder room/shower. These 'wet areas' link to a new galley-style kitchen that forms part of the dining and living areas. "It's a relatively long space, so we divided the kitchen into a number of functional parts," says interior designer Sioux Clark, co-director of the practice. These parts include the laundry at one end of the kitchen, a scullery, and a pantry. These functions, clad in blackheart-sassafras timber, have a graphic presence.

One of the things missing in the original design was texture. There was no point of difference

On the other side of the kitchen is a long bench with a citrus-yellow glass splashback, separating the lower cupboards made from black laminate from the timber cupboards above. Concealed fluorescent lighting illuminates the glass, magnifying a reflection of the garden views. Central to the kitchen is a bench made of black laminate and steel legs. To create a slightly aged patina, panels from the 1950s were used as drawer fronts. "One of the things missing in the original design was texture. There was no point of difference," says O'Sullivan.

To further animate the kitchen and living areas, a number of alcoves in the ceiling were created, allowing the design to move away from its rectilinear form. Adding a sense of playfulness to the design, the architects created a whimsical 1970s-inspired courtyard. Green nylon was finely woven to create a balustrade to a deck for the children to play on. Built-in seating in the courtyard allows the parents to enjoy the garden rather than simply viewing it through narrow windows.

We designed the house so that it could be used by several members of the family at the same time

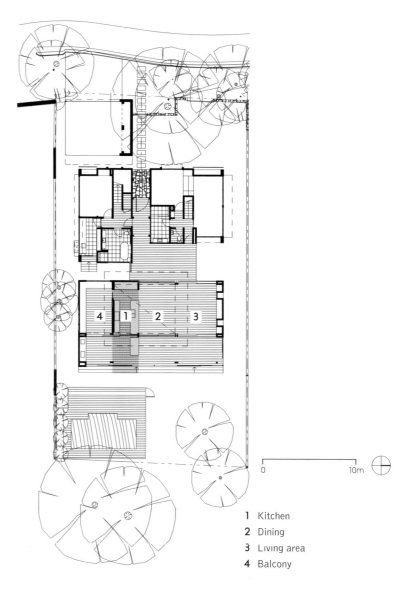

DESIGNED FOR AN EXTENDED family that spans three generations, this weekender enjoys views over sand dunes and rolling lawns. "We designed the house so that it could be used by several members of the family at the same time," says architect Paul Uhlmann, who included two separate bedroom pavilions and a spacious open-plan kitchen, living and dining area. **>>**

1 Kitchen
2 Dining
3 Living area
4 Balcony

The open-plan kitchen and living areas are connected to a terrace spanning the entire width of the home. To make the most of the outside area the design incorporates two tiers of doors—large sliding doors on the edge of the living areas that can be pulled back into cavity walls, and a second series of doors, made from stainless-steel mesh and timber, that can be left closed if the owners are at the beach. "We used these mesh doors for a number of reasons. They're security doors, but we're also in a bushfire zone," says Uhlmann. "The other issue here is insects, such as mosquitoes," he adds.

The kitchen, which is split between the inside and outside areas, features one continuous bench. With a spotted-gum benchtop and two-pack painted cupboards, it's a relaxed and informal arrangement. "We've used green marble as a feature wall for additional surface interest," says Uhlmann. Notable in the design is the change in ceiling heights between the indoor and outdoor kitchen, changing from 3.8 metres inside to 2.7 metres on the terrace. "We wanted to bring additional light into the kitchen and living areas," says Uhlmann, pointing out the highlight windows.

The kitchen is also a buffer zone between the children's play area on one side and the dining and living areas on the other, however, the entire family is regularly found eating on the terrace. The outdoor kitchen features a barbeque and sink, as well as a bar fridge and storage space, including an area for wine. "And if insects are a problem, then it's just a matter of closing these screens," adds Uhlmann.

One of the other changes made was to the building's layout, creating two courtyards

THIS DOUBLE-FRONTED VICTORIAN terrace originally had the usual additions tacked on the rear. "In the Victorian period the kitchen and service areas were the last to be considered in a building's hierarchy," says architect Ian Perkins. "The original kitchen also created an obstruction to the garden."

Perkins removed the lean-to and added a new kitchen and dining area together with a separate living area and a study. One of the other changes made was to the building's layout, creating two courtyards, one to the rear and the other to one side of the house. "The courtyards create acoustic privacy from neighbours," says Perkins, who dulled the sound further by including two ponds in one of the courtyards.

The main courtyard leads from the kitchen and dining area, and is protected by a timber-batten ceiling below a clear-polycarbonate roof. To ensure it's used for alfresco dining, Perkins included a built-in barbeque. "Our clients can simply move a table through the glass doors, together with a few chairs," says Perkins, who also included built-in banquette-style seating.

The kitchen and dining area in the house were conceived as one space. The kitchen joinery, for example, made from MDF with a two-pack-paint finish, extends into the dining area to create a credenza. Reconstituted-stone benches extend the entire width of the room. "We're seeing more kitchens being integrated into dining areas," says Perkins. However, while there is a dining table, there is also a 1.2-metre-wide island bench in the kitchen that can be used for informal meals.

Like dining areas, kitchens are also becoming more refined. For this kitchen Perkins designed built-in shelving next to the pantry for the owners to display objects and artifacts. The open shelves, made from MDF, are framed by glass walls and are backlit. "The light naturally illuminates the objects during the day," says Perkins, who added a shimmer to the interior by waxing the walls.

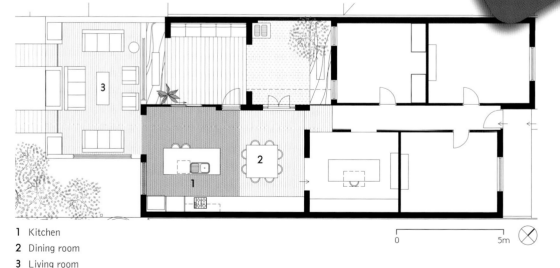

1 Kitchen
2 Dining room
3 Living room

0   5m

The kitchen and living areas are the most used parts of the house

with sink and a second dishwasher. Rather than conceal food behind closed doors, as in the main kitchen, open timber shelves provide convenient access.

To the other side of the kitchen is a space where the children can do their homework or spread out their artwork. Although it can be closed off with a sliding door, it is usually left open, allowing for parental supervision.

With these ancillary spaces there was plenty of room for a large island bench made from Carrara marble. Set on lightly polished concrete floors that extend to the dining and living areas, this bench can remain free of clutter. "The kitchen and living areas are the most used parts of the house. It made sense to locate these to maximise the light," adds Swansson.

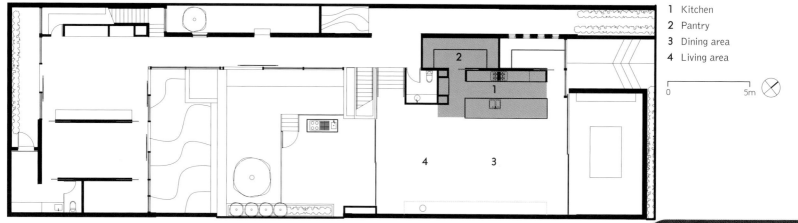

1 Kitchen
2 Pantry
3 Dining area
4 Living area

0   5m

THIS NEW TWO-STOREY family home enjoys light-filled views to the street. Rather than turn its back to the light, architect Richard Swansson designed the kitchen, dining, and living areas at the front of the house. To create privacy, the house was elevated above a basement garage, and a moveable screen made from cane was included across a front window.

The kitchen, which forms part of the dining and living areas, features acacia-veneer joinery that has been waxed. Complemented with a Carrara marble splash-back and stainless-steel benches, it's a low-maintenance design for a couple with three children. While the kitchen appears modest in size, it conceals two rooms on either side of the joinery. To one side, via a sliding door, is a walk-in pantry. There's also a kitchenette,

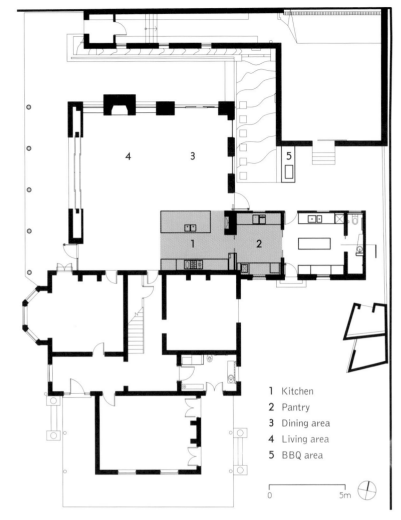

1 Kitchen
2 Pantry
3 Dining area
4 Living area
5 BBQ area

0   5m

While the owners enjoy entertaining indoors, weather doesn't prevent them from preparing meals outside

THIS LARGE VICTORIAN VILLA required significant work to be recreated into a family home. While there were more than sufficient rooms, many of the spaces, including the kitchen, required an overhaul. One the main changes in the renovation was to create large open-plan kitchen and informal living areas. As the kitchen forms part of the living areas, architect Richard Swansson created a 'back of house' kitchen as well. "When you're designing a kitchen for a family, you need to anticipate the mess," says Swansson. >>

The main kitchen features joinery made from hand-pressed acacia veneer, which was customised by furniture designer Damian Wright. Behind this joinery is the fridge, together with generous storage. Swansson used stainless steel for the benchtop and green glass for the splashback. Central to the design of the kitchen is an off-formed-concrete island bench, poured in situ. "I wanted to create something quite monumental. The concrete complements the timber floors," says Swansson. As the preparation areas are to one side of the kitchen, the island bench can remain free of clutter and dishes.

'Back of house' has been thoughtfully considered. This area includes a scullery, a pantry, sinks and preparation areas. Leading from the scullery is a laundry. "It means the owners can put on a load of washing while they're starting to think about dinner," says Swansson.

While many homes have an outdoor area for entertaining, this house includes two outdoor areas for cooking. There's a barbeque in the courtyard adjacent to the scullery that is used by the family for everyday meals. There's also a large off-formed-concrete pavilion. Open on the sides and framed by two layers of curtains (fabric for summer and plastic for winter), this pavilion features a garden on its roof.

"As you can see the roof of the pavilion from the first floor, it was important to green it," says Swansson, who worked closely with landscape architect Tim Nicholas. While the owners enjoy entertaining indoors, weather doesn't prevent them from preparing meals outside.

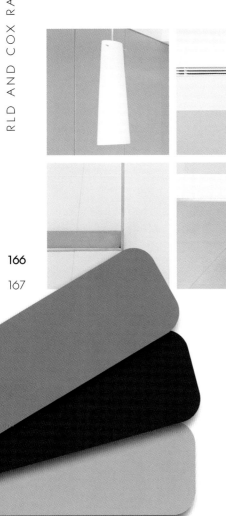

THIS DEVELOPMENT BY STOCKLAND comprises a number of apartments, penthouses, villa units and detached homes. RLD worked closely with Cox Rayner Architects in creating streamlined contemporary interiors for this high-end development. "We wanted to give people a number of options. Aesthetics, as well as function, drove each design," says Andrea D'Cruz, co-director of RLD.

The kitchens in each dwelling are slightly different, both in layout and materials used. This kitchen, located in one of the detached homes, features limestone flooring throughout and open-plan living areas. The kitchen is sleek and minimal and includes an island bench finished in reconstituted stone. At one end of the island bench is a sink, with generous storage below. And at the other end, the benchtop extends to form a table for informal dining. Rather than clutter the space with heavy legs, the table features folded stainless steel. "The feeling is light and transparent," says D'Cruz.

The kitchen also features a bank of polyurethane cupboards in a taupe colour, together with polyurethane white drawers that extend to form a credenza in the living areas. To help define the kitchen, as well as concealing the air-conditioning unit, a bulkhead was placed over the kitchen area. Lit from above by fluorescent lighting, the ceiling appears to float.

A pantry is located at the furthest end of the kitchen providing storage for food as well as concealing household appliances. "When you're designing open-plan kitchens, you don't want to see clutter from the living areas," says D'Cruz, who also included a butler's pantry (concealed kitchenettes) in many of the homes on this development. Whether or not there is a butler's pantry, each kitchen design by D'Cruz follows the triangular principle – the food-storage, preparation and cooking areas are arranged in this shape. "A kitchen has to be functional, irrespective of its size," she adds.

Aesthetics, as well as function, drove each design

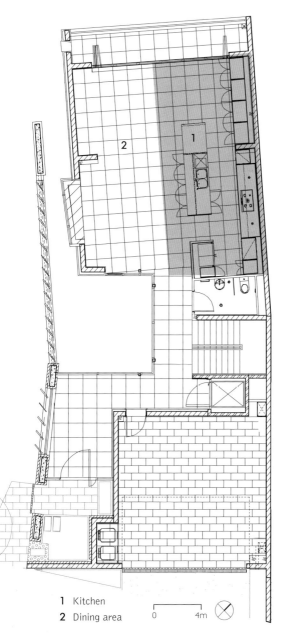

1 Kitchen
2 Dining area

0   4m

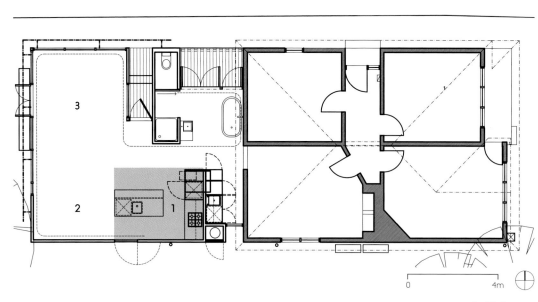

To create a greater sense of internalised space, white cotton curtains are used along the full extent of the window wall

1 Kitchen
2 Dining area
3 Living area

THIS EDWARDIAN-STYLE TIMBER home had a serene feel to it from the initial inspection by architect Robert Simeoni. "There was a certain softness to the interior. It had a real spirit about it," says Simeoni, who was keen to develop a sense of how his client lived in the house.

While the original part of the house, comprising four rooms—two on either side of a corridor—needed little work, the rear section required reworking. "There was a 1930s lean-to. It was fairly small and inadequate for contemporary living," says Simeoni, who replaced the lean-to with a timber-frame structure clad in western red cedar. Featuring several "cut-out" windows, the new wing is now directly linked to its garden setting. **>>**

The addition comprises an open-plan kitchen, dining and living areas. Rather than conceal the bathroom, Simeoni located it behind a white cotton curtain. "The claw-foot bath came from the original bathroom," says Simeoni. "We sought to create an integral visual feature of the new design where kitchen, bathroom, and living areas are visually interconnected and separated only by curtains so as to create an ambiguity of space," he adds.

The kitchen features white laminate cupboards and carrara marble benchtops. With a concealed fridge the island bench is the only distinct form in the kitchen. It features laminate cupboards and a marble benchtop. Lights from Artemides, located above the island bench, are the few deliberate decorative elements of the kitchen.

To facilitate privacy from neighbours, and to create a greater sense of internalised space, white cotton curtains are used along the full extent of the window wall and gathered along one kitchen wall. An openable window hatch has been located so as to capture cooler summer breezes to ensure good cross ventilation. "It's a modest and practical kitchen, with the island bench positioned orthogonally to the main orientation thereby creating a more abstract composition," says Simeoni. Before the kitchen was enclosed, now it's integral to the living spaces.

THE KITCHEN REPLACES A smaller kitchen in an existing house. The dwelling forms part of a residential and office complex designed in the late 1990s by an architect known for crafting visually complex compositions using a wide range of commonly used materials. The existing kitchen, while forming an integral part of the whole, was in need of upgrading. In its original location adjacent to the entry, it obscured views of the living area and limited the ingress of light from a series of attractive windows on the east wall.

Consequently the new kitchen has been placed at the far corner of the room and although much larger has, as a result of its placement, not impinged on the feeling of space within the room. The living space is divided into two levels, the higher level being extended to allow the kitchen to remain at the entry level. In this location the kitchen addresses the entry and living areas and is better connected to the rear courtyard thus promoting its active use.

The form of the kitchen and the materials used are purposely restrained to limit the visual impact of the kitchen within the original space. The relative neutrality of the cabinetwork allows the more decorative features of the original interior to predominate thus permitting the old to happily coexist with the new. **>>**

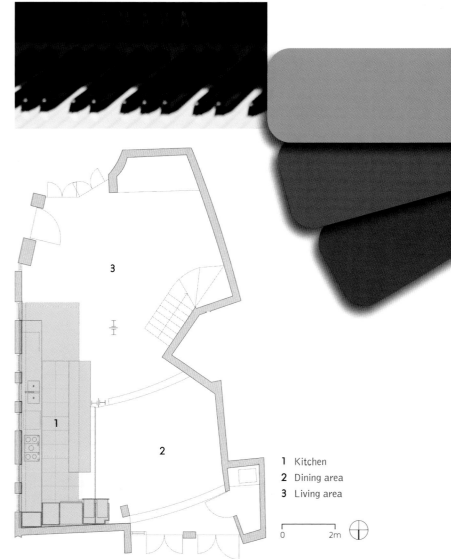

The existing kitchen, while forming an integral part of the whole, was in need of upgrading

1 Kitchen
2 Dining area
3 Living area

0   2m

The cabinetwork has been arranged as a simple composition of rectangular prisms each constructed with materials particular to their form and function. The island bench is a combination of white lacquer and Statuario Venato marble. The main workbench with the cooktop and sinks uses the same white lacquer coupled with white Corian. The tall cupboard housing the refrigerator, wall oven and pantry is finished in white lacquer. The exhaust hood is housed in a rectangular timber-veneer box suspended from the ceiling. Air conditioning and lighting are effectively housed in a new dropped ceiling that extends from the entry and over the area of the kitchen.

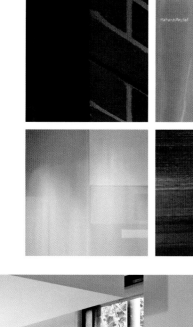

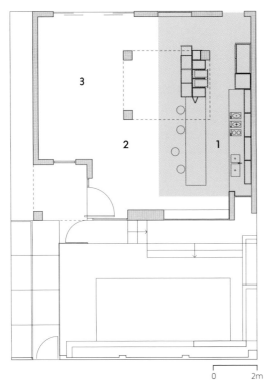

1 Kitchen
2 Dining room
3 Living room

0   2m

The kitchen is simply delineated from the living areas by a large central island

THIS HOUSE WAS ORIGINALLY built in the 1980s and although it was structurally sound, the kitchen and living areas occupied a relatively small footprint. "The original kitchen was quite small. The most impressive thing was the ceiling heights," says architect Simon Rodrigues, a co-director of Rodrigues Bodycoat Architecture. "The proportions were odd and there was no connection to the garden." **>>**

The architects designed spacious new kitchen, dining and living areas at the rear of the house. With generous glazing and doors, this area is now used as the main point of entry into the home. The kitchen is simply delineated from the living areas by a large central island, featuring a dusty-grey reconstituted-stone benchtop. Rather than include cupboards below the bench, the architects designed an extensive bank of drawers. With flush-extruded aluminium handles, these drawers appear streamlined. "We find our clients prefer the drawer system, rather than cupboards. They're slightly more expensive to install, but you can pull them out and see where everything is," says Rodrigues.

While there are numerous drawers in the kitchen, there is also a pull-out pantry adjacent to the island bench, along with an appliance cupboard. "A kitchen design usually starts with a list of appliances, either owned or intended to be bought by the client. Some prefer wall ovens, others prefer below-bench," says Rodrigues, who sees a need to create a balance between bench space and joinery.

Among the unusual features in this kitchen are the bronze and mirrored display cabinets used for wine storage. Capable of holding up to 80 bottles, the cabinets also double as a splashback. "The owner saw a glazed walk-in wine cellar in another house with a similar display system, but they didn't want to reduce the floor area for their kitchen," says Rodrigues.

1 Kitchen area
2 Dining area
3 Living area

0   5m

Inspiration was provided by the clients' fondness for the pool areas they experienced in various hotels and resorts around the world

IN A SUBURB NORTHWEST of Sydney this unique resort-style property is hidden from the everyday chaos by a backdrop of natural bush. Inspiration for the garden and entertainment areas was provided by the client's fondness for the pool areas they experienced in various hotels and resorts around the world.

"The garden presented an opportunity to recreate resort-style living for a private property," says landscape designer Dean Herald. "The overall size and scale of the pool and pavilion had to be in keeping with the rest of the property and presented an excellent opportunity to explore the use of space and the function of certain areas." **>>**

The blue-tiled pool with a wet-edge spillover extends out towards the bush. The pool's natural lagoon shape with its generous curves creates a sense of tranquillity. Incorporated into the pool is a glass-sided spa that has an uninterrupted connection with the entertainment pavilion.

It is in the entertainment pavilion that the hosts and their guests best interact. A cantilevered roof provides protection for the cooking, dining, and relaxation areas. A fully independent outdoor kitchen – which includes a teppanyaki-style barbeque, sink, integrated fridge and ample storage space – ensures that there is no need for the hosts to continually go inside the house for supplies. The dining area is positioned close to the kitchen so there is no separation between the hosts and their guests. An outdoor fireplace with a stone-clad chimney is surrounded by a lounge, ensuring that the pavilion and entertainment area can be used year round.

On the lower level to the pavilion is a swim-up bar containing a curved stainless-steel ice trough for storing drinks. Stainless-steel stools provide an opportunity for those in the pool to relax and enjoy a drink without having to leave the water.

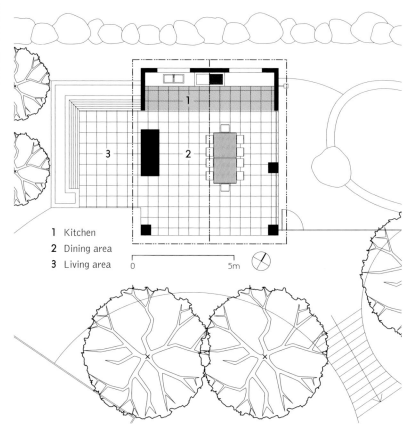

1 Kitchen
2 Dining area
3 Living area

0   5m

The owners required a space to entertain away from their busy lives

CAREFUL CONSIDERATION WAS REQUIRED when designing this pavilion in Sydney's northwest. Alpine stone and Australian hardwood were selected to ensure that the structure blended into its natural bush surroundings. The owners required a space to entertain away from their busy lives and engaged landscape designer Dean Herald to create something special. "I was provided with a brief to design a structure that was multi-use and would connect the home, tennis court and pool," says Herald.

The pavilion's form and style has been created using coloured stone and the rich browns of Australian hardwood while making use of the natural light that complements the materials' colours, textures and angles. Picture windows around the kitchen are framed with wide hardwood boards and the roof is covered with Woodland Grey Colorbond sheeting. **>>**

A large double-sided fireplace divides the entertainment area into two. Outside the pavilion, coming off the fireplace, is a lounge area. Timber benches surround the fireplace and are supported behind by raised planter boxes, which help to create a sense of intimacy. Inside the pavilion there is a 6-metre-long custom-built kitchen bench that includes a sink, barbecue, integrated fridge, dishwasher and storage cupboards. "The client wanted to have an independent outdoor kitchen," says Dean. A fireplace with a feature wood stack warms the dining area during the cooler nights and also assists in making the area more comfortable during winter.

Also included in the pavilion is a plasma television and surround-sound audio equipment. This, in association with the other items, provides a fantastic space for the owners to entertain and relax with family and friends in a picturesque bush setting.

Contemporary gardens can be functional, fun and the perfect place to relax

1 Kitchen
2 Dining area
3 Living area

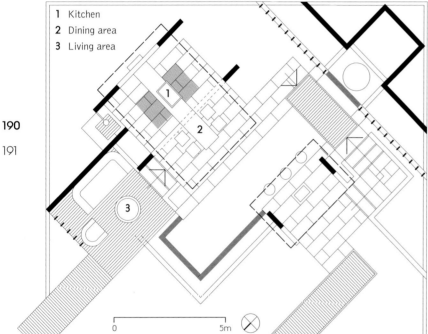

0   5m

THE ANNUAL MELBOURNE International Flower and Garden Show (MIFGS), considered to be one of the top five garden shows in the world, is located in the picturesque inner-city Carlton Gardens. MIFGS showcases designer gardens with the latest trends in outdoor design. In 2007 Dean Herald, director and principal designer of Rolling Stone Landscapes, created a display at the MIFGS that showed how contemporary gardens can be functional, fun and the perfect place to relax.

The centrepiece of Herald's lavish resort-style design is a fully tiled lap pool, around which all the surrounding spaces comfortably mesh. The 10-metre-long wet-edge pool includs a swim-up wet bar complete with stainless-steel stools and a custom-made bar that conveniently contained a fridge, sink and storage area.

Adjacent to the lap pool is a cooking and dining pavilion that features a multipurpose handcrafted floating kitchen. The 5-metre-long Corian counter is suspended from the ceiling with a dining table at one end and a cooking station at the other. The counter's sleek lines and clean styling epitomise the calibre of design expected in a luxury resort landscape. This clever design creates the opportunity for the host to interact with the guests even while preparing a meal.

Down from the cooking and dining area is a timber deck that supports the lounge area. From here the entire pool area and garden can be viewed. It is the seamless connection between the various areas of Herald's garden that demonstrates how a good design can create an entertainment paradise for all to enjoy.

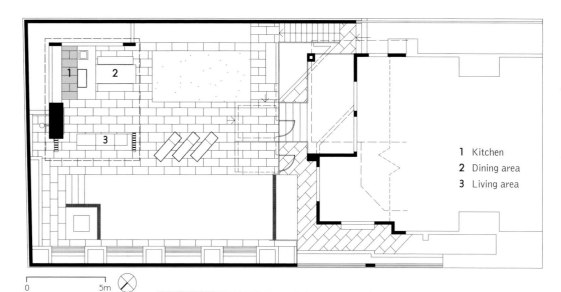

1 Kitchen
2 Dining area
3 Living area

0   5m

The outdoor kitchen included a teppanyaki-style barbeque, pizza oven, sink and custom-made fridge

ONE OF THE MOST common briefs received by a landscape designer is to create an area that is suitable for entertaining family and friends alike. Designer Dean Herald embraced this brief from his clients and created an entertainment paradise suited to their needs. Having designed six award-winning show gardens, Herald has enjoyed transforming the idea of a garden from simply being visually pleasing into a space that can be lived in and enjoyed year round.

A blue Bisazza-tiled pool, located on the western side of the backyard, forms an elegant feature that includes a tiled wet-edge spillover. This creates a soothing outlook for the billiard room on the lower level. A glass spa is cleverly positioned to catch glimpses of the Sydney Harbour Bridge, and the spa is close enough to the main pavilion to ensure that people in it are connected to those cooking or enjoying the lounge.

The main pavilion has been designed with entertaining in mind. The outdoor kitchen includes a teppanyaki-style barbeque, pizza oven, sink and custom-made fridge. A unique cantilevered dining table has been incorporated into the kitchen bench that extends out towards the buffalo lawn and ensures that the connection between the cooks and their guests is always maintained. A fireplace allows the pavilion to be more accommodating during the cooler months.

The clever use of space and the connection between different areas of the garden help to create a relaxing environment for the owners and their guests. This tailor-made backyard is not only a joy to look at but has been designed for maximum use.

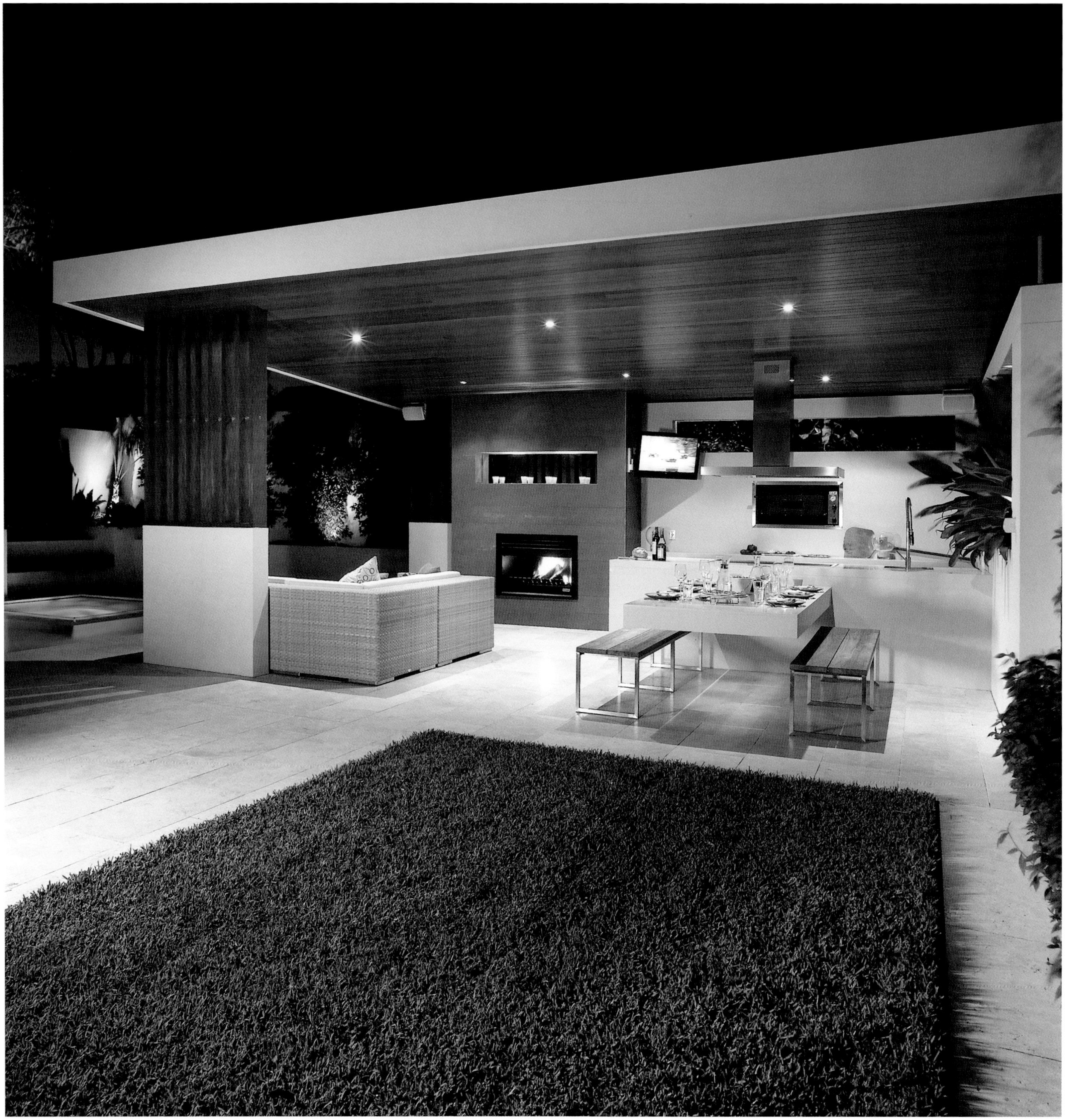

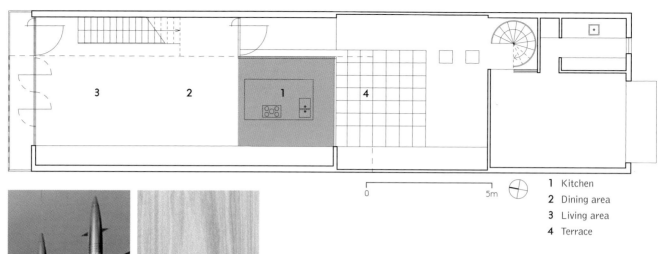

1	Kitchen
2	Dining area
3	Living area
4	Terrace

It's a narrow space, so it was important to build in as much furniture as possible

THIS HOUSE HAS THE typology of a terrace, but it's a completely new home. "Originally, there was a single-storey Victorian cottage on the site, but it was completely dilapidated," says architect Matthew Chan, director of Scale Architecture.

While the house is new, the width of the site (6.5 metres) couldn't be altered. To compensate for this, Chan dispensed with the usual corridor associated with a Victorian terrace. The front door opens to reveal an open-plan kitchen, living and dining area. Instead of a corridor, visitors are greeted by a staircase, made from timber treads and supported by steel rods.

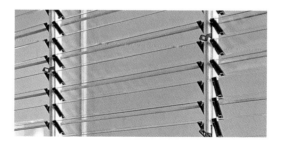

There is a central island bench in the kitchen. Constructed in off-formed concrete, the bench appears as an extension of the concrete floors. Measuring 1.4 metres wide by 2.2 metres long, the bench, with double stainless-steel sinks, appears monolithic. "It was designed to take pride of place. It's the place where people tend to gather, whether it's the owners or their friends," says Chan. >>

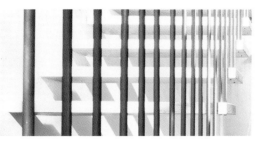

The other main feature of the kitchen is walnut-veneer joinery that extends almost the entire width of the kitchen and living areas (approximately 12 metres in length). Concealing the fridge, pantry and laundry, these cupboards also contain an area for wine storage (adjacent to the dining area). In the living room this joinery incorporates the television set, the hi-fi system, and a storage area. "It's a narrow space, so it was important to build in as much furniture as possible," says Chan.

One of the other features of the kitchen is a wall of louvred-glass windows that open to a small pond and draw moist air through the kitchen and living room. "The fresh air cools down the place, particularly during the warmer months, as well as filtering the odours from cooking."

The new angular roof above the kitchen, dining, and informal living areas was the driving force in the design of the kitchen

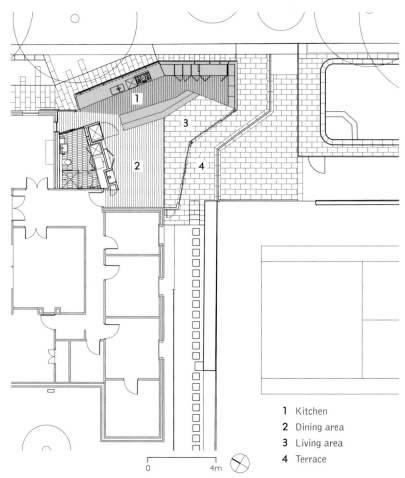

1 Kitchen
2 Dining area
3 Living area
4 Terrace

0   4m

THIS CALIFORNIA BUNGALOW was in reasonably good condition when Terroir first inspected it. While the house required a little updating, it was the kitchen that required most attention. "Essentially, we only demolished the kitchen and laundry. The additional space is no more than 45 square metres," says architect Allison Earl.

To compensate for the low level of light entering the kitchen, the architects designed an angled roof, elevated above celestial windows. "Our clients wanted us to open the kitchen to the swimming pool and tennis court (both existing). They also wanted us to create an outdoor area where they could dine," says Earl.

The new angular roof above the kitchen, dining, and informal living areas was the driving force in the design of the kitchen joinery. Angular kitchen cupboards, made from MDF and painted a high-gloss white, create a boomerang-shape. Separating the kitchen from the dining area is an angular-shaped island bench. This bench features a stone top, with jarrah-veneer joinery drawers cantilevered above. "There are drawers on the dining side for cutlery," says Earl, who also included open shelves on the side of the dining area, and large drawers on the kitchen side to store pots and pans. **>>**

A wall of shelves in the dining area also forms part of the kitchen joinery. As well as cupboards and open shelves to display objects, there is a fridge concealed behind a door that is also made from MDF. To create warmth in the open-plan area a gas-fire heater was included within the joinery.

As the brief included strengthening the connection to the outdoors, the dining area's tiled floor was extended to the terrace. Located beyond large glass sliding doors, there's a gentle transition between the indoor and outdoor spaces. "The joinery was deliberately finished in high-gloss paint. We wanted to bring the reflections of the garden inside," says Earl.

It's a dark palette, but it's highly reflective

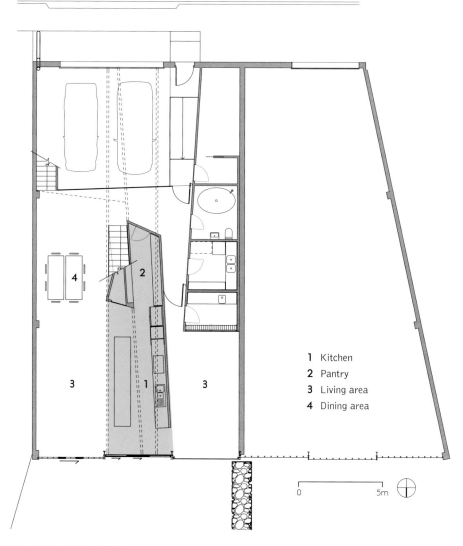

1 Kitchen
2 Pantry
3 Living area
4 Dining area

0   5m

AFTER PURCHASING THIS 1970S warehouse, architect Scott Balmforth, a director of Terroir, subdivided it in two. As the warehouse features generous ceiling heights, varying from 5 to 6.5 metres, he was able to create a mezzanine level in each home. "We've actually ended up with more space," says Balmforth, who lives here with his partner and their three children.

Balmforth gutted the warehouse and created an open-plan kitchen, dining and living area. The kitchen, located to one side of this space, is nestled below the mezzanine level. The mezzanine level contains the bedrooms, as well as a study, and is faced in expanded metal sheets. "The metal allows views out rather than in," says Balmforth. **>>**

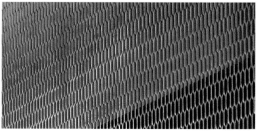

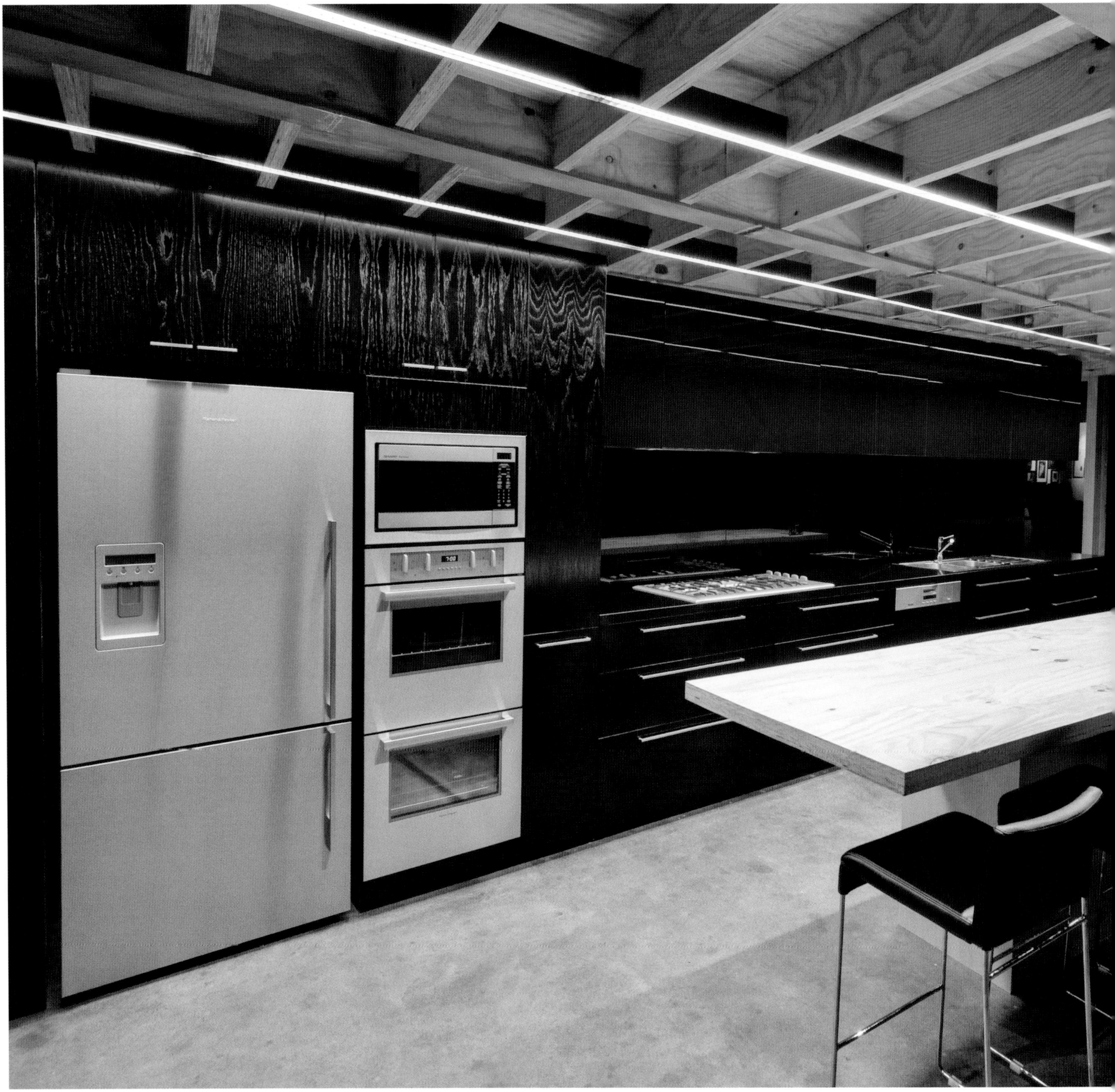

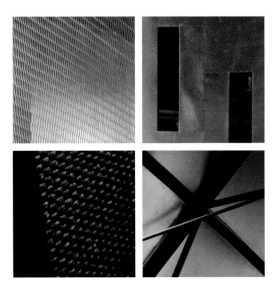

The kitchen, like the living areas, features original concrete that has been cleaned and sealed. Instead of a traditional island bench, there is a 4.8-metre-long table made from plywood and laminated together. "The table is the hub of the house. It's where the meals are prepared, as well as being used for children's homework," says Balmforth. "It's the place where people gather." The long galley-style kitchen features exposed plywood beams, delineated with black steel beams and strip fluorescent lighting. "The ceiling height in the kitchen is only 2.2 metres, so I couldn't include pendant lighting," says Balmforth.

While the kitchen joinery, made from American oak, appears like a simple black wall, it has been cleverly designed to reveal a number of subtle textures. "I used the oak because it shows its grain, even after being painted," says Balmforth, who included black mirror on the front of the overhead cupboards. There's also a black glass splashback. "It's a dark palette, but it's highly reflective," says Balmforth, who wanted to capture reflections of the adjacent courtyard-style garden.

The courtyard, with a gabion wall, is accessed via glass sliding doors. Balmforth also retained an original steel sliding door in the design, punctuating it with small windows to allow additional light to penetrate. "We often dine in the courtyard. It's really an extension of the kitchen," he adds.

The kitchen needed to exist as a large piece of bespoke furniture that would not degrade the sense of a high-quality living and dining space

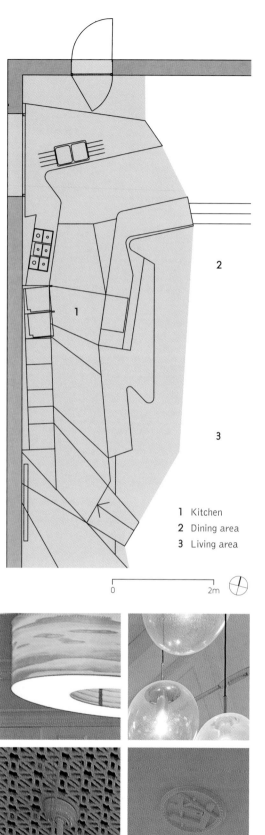

1 Kitchen
2 Dining area
3 Living area

0   2m

THE SITE FOR THIS project was a Masonic Club hall located within a suburban context that the client wanted to convert into a single-occupant house. The scale of the internal volumes of the hall presented unique challenges in terms of the proposed use, and the need to address these challenges defined the design approach.

The key strategy was to maintain the quality of the existing spaces via a strategy of discrete insertions into the hall to enable domestic occupation while also minimising unnecessary energy use by capturing different activities in small spaces. These insertions take the occupant from the large halls further and further into an 'interior' until, unexpectedly, they press against the exterior surface and break through to the garden, giving the occupant an external aspect. **>>**

This strategy was carried over to the kitchen, which had to sit within the largest space along with living and dining functions. Given that the clients bought the building for the elegant scale and materiality of this space – and were to furnish it with 20th-century timber Danish furniture – the kitchen presented a problem in terms of compromising this with industrial finishes and overt displays of technology. Rather, the kitchen needed to exist as a large piece of bespoke furniture that would not degrade the sense of a high-quality living and dining space.

Inspired by the Danish furniture being purchased, the kitchen was designed as a substantial timber object with a fluid form that negotiates various functions such as workbench, servery and informal eating area. By paying careful attention to the timber selection and detailing, the main bench has the appearance of a solid element that addresses these functions without resorting to standard fittings or finishes. Similarly, a timber joinery unit runs along the wall behind this bench with the only visible fitments being two ovens.

The result is a kitchen that not only complements, but completes an elegant living–dining space by conceiving the kitchen not as work centre replete with technology and industrial finishes, but a sensuous and substantial piece of furniture.

While the kitchen is
compact, it enjoys
extended views
through a large
picture window

3 2 4 1

0   5m

1 Kitchen
2 Dining area
3 Courtyard
4 Living area

THIS FEDERATION-STYLE TERRACE (circa 1900)
had been added to over the years. A kitchen had been
tacked on, and there was still an outside toilet. "The
house was in fairly poor condition," says designer Matt
Krusin of Tobias Partners. "But on the positive side, it
was a fairly long site (approximately 33 metres) for the
inner city," he adds.

As well as removing the additions, the house was
gutted, and to create more space a first floor was added,
including a main bedroom, ensuite and walk-in dressing
area. "We only retained the first two rooms, one of
which is now used as a bedroom and the other is a
bathroom," says Krusin. >>

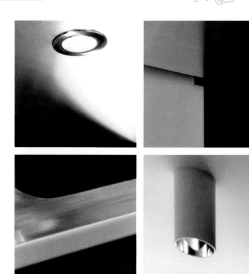

As the site falls approximately 3 metres from the street, the designers were able to create double-height spaces in the new kitchen and open-plan living areas. "We lowered the ceiling over the dining area to provide cross-ventilation," says Krusin, pointing out the louvred blinds above the dining area.

The kitchen benefits from the double-height space, because although the galley-style kitchen isn't large it features generous cupboards above the bench. "Our client is a collector, so storage was crucial," says Krusin. Made from a dark-grey laminate, the kitchen cupboards appear to wrap around the central joinery unit. To add depth, as well as creating additional storage, Tobias Partners created an alcove of stainless steel within the laminate joinery. There is a stainless-steel benchtop, as well as a stainless-steel 'ceiling' within the alcove, and what appears to be a stainless-steel splashback is actually two sliding cupboards that open to reveal laminate shelves.

While the kitchen is compact, it enjoys extended views through a large picture window to a courtyard. This courtyard is lined with crushed white gravel and is planted with a singular pear tree. A timber deck leading from the living area provides additional outdoor space. Located above the garage, this deck is used for casual dining.

When you're designing kitchens in small spaces, every centimetre counts

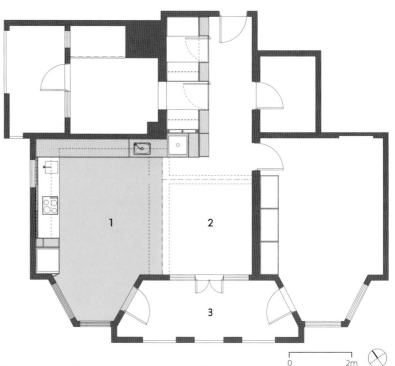

THIS OLDER STYLE APARTMENT has been completely reworked by Tribe Studio. One of the major alterations was relocating the kitchen. "Originally, the kitchen was enclosed in a small room. That room is now a child's bedroom," says architect and studio manager Josephine Hurley. The kitchen now forms part of the open-plan living areas.

To maximise space the island bench was removed. Most of the kitchen is concealed behind slender bi-fold doors which also conceal the laundry and additional storage. The working kitchen features black laminate cupboards and black laminate shelving for crockery and glasses, together with generous bench space.

The exposed kitchen, which features white polyurethane cupboards and a white reconstituted-stone benchtop, includes the stove, oven and sink. One of the problems encountered in the renovation, apart from the usual plumbing issues, was the apartment's sill height – the new bench was higher than the sills. The solution was to create a mesh stainless-steel screen that moves on a sliding track to allow the window to be opened. "The screen filters the light, as well as providing a splashback," says Hurley. **>>**

0   2m

1 Kitchen/Dining
2 Living area
3 Balcony

As the apartment is relatively modest in scale, the architect created the one dining area, loosely defined by the coffered ceiling. "We removed a wall in the living area to open up the entire space. Some of these ceiling beams form part of the original structure. Other beams (made of plaster) have been added," says Hurley, who was also keen to add visual interest in the design.

Although the finishes and materials are modest, the kitchen is highly functional. "When you're designing kitchens in small spaces, every centimetre counts," says Hurley.

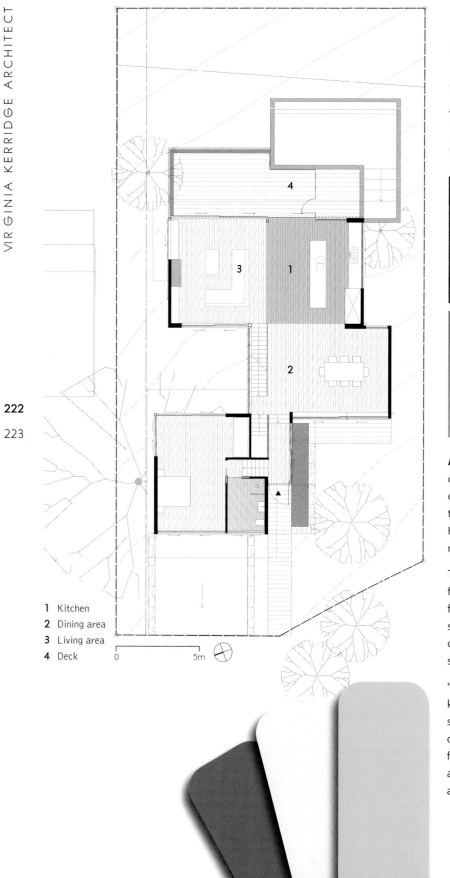

1 Kitchen
2 Dining area
3 Living area
4 Deck

0   5m

It's not always about creating a statement that screams for attention

A VACANT SITE ALONG the coast is like a blank canvas for an architect. Without the planning constraints on building found in the city, creating that 'one out of the box' design is a possibility. But as architect Virginia Kerridge says, "It's not always about creating a statement that screams for attention."

This coastal house is quietly constrained. Constructed from a steel frame and clad in timber and compressed fibre-cement sheets, the house is stepped across the sloping site. Kerridge draws you into the house from a covered timber walkway, flanked by a pond edged in sandstone.

"The entrance is slightly compressed, making the kitchen and living areas feel considerably larger," she says. While the kitchen, dining and living areas are open plan, they are loosely delineated by timber battens framing the staircase. "We wanted to keep the areas as transparent as possible, allowing the views, as well as the sea breezes, to filter through," says Kerridge. **>>**

Large sliding doors across the kitchen and living areas can be pulled back to form a continuous space with the outdoor deck and pool. At the front of the house, there is the option of opening a sliding door to the dining area or drawing across a timber batten screen. Made from blackbutt, the screen conceals a bronze mesh layer to prevent insects entering the kitchen, while providing security at the same time.

The kitchen is relaxed. The island bench is clad in timber, like the flooring throughout the house. Stainless-steel benchtops and polyurethane cupboards are easily wiped down. And while there's a dining table, the owners have informal meals sitting at the bench, which cantilevers at one end.

The architect was also mindful of cross-ventilation and to allow air to channel through the kitchen from the pond on one side and the swimming pool on the other. "We wanted to use the water around the house to cool the place down in the summer months. The sound of water also provides a calming backdrop when you're in the kitchen preparing food," she adds.

This house is about enjoying the outdoors, whether you're in the kitchen or lying in bed having breakfast

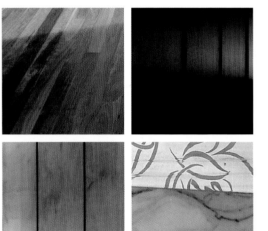

THIS HOUSE APPEARS AS A SINGLE storey from the street, but as the site falls away 5 metres it actually becomes a two-storey structure. Constructed of insulated concrete panels and clad in western red cedar (stained ebony), the house was designed for a couple scaling down in their latter years. "The first floor was designed like a luxury apartment. The couple can live in the upstairs and close off the entire ground floor," says architect Jeremy Wolveridge. "The rooms downstairs (bedrooms and rumpus room) were primarily designed for the children and grandchildren," he adds.

Originally, there was a tennis court on site. This has been retained, with the new house overlooking the court and adjacent golf links. On the first floor of the house are the main bedroom and ensuite. An open-plan kitchen, dining and living areas designed with grand proportions – 12 metres long by 7 metres wide – and to extend the space even further, a large deck wraps around the kitchen and living areas. **>>**

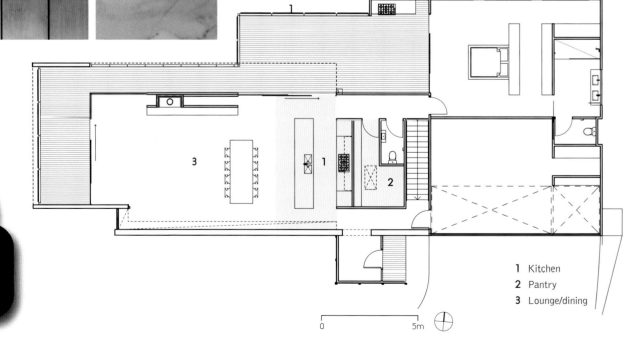

1 Kitchen
2 Pantry
3 Lounge/dining

0　　　　5m

Wolveridge designed the kitchen like an altarpiece. A free-standing unit is clad in stained-timber veneer, with generous storage space. This joinery conceals a fridge on one side and storage area on the other. Behind this unit is also a walk-in pantry, together with a separate powder room.

To lighten the expanse of timber, a lively splashback was inserted and wallpaper was inserted behind the glass. The architects also included a large island bench in the kitchen. Made from Calacatta marble with a gold vein running through it, the bench is almost 5 metres long.

While the kitchen was designed for entertaining on the grand scale, there is also a built-in barbeque on the deck adjacent to the kitchen. To ensure that food circled the house, the architects created access to the deck from the main bedroom. "This house is about enjoying the outdoors, whether you're in the kitchen or lying in bed having breakfast," adds Wolveridge.

THIS SPACIOUS HOME WAS designed as a far northern getaway for three families. As a result, there are four bedrooms, two of which are main bedrooms with ensuites. "I was inspired by the work of Geoffrey Bawa (Sri Lankan architect). He was practising in the 1960s and 70s," says architect Jeremy Wolveridge. "It's a fusion of indigenous and contemporary design."

The kitchen, living and dining areas are located on the ground floor of the house. To reach these, there are a series of boardwalks (timber decks that are partially covered). One of the most used parts of the house is the outdoor dining area, adjacent to the kitchen and living areas. "There's no formal dining area. There's just the one meals area, and it's fully covered," says Wolveridge. >>

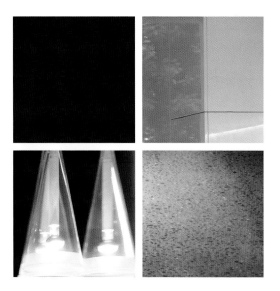

It's a fusion of indigenous and contemporary design

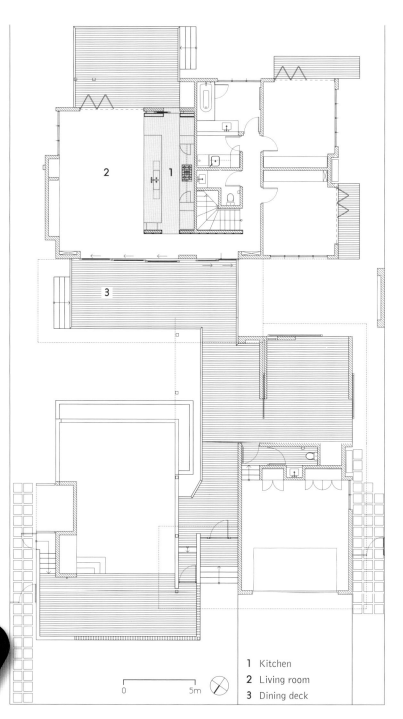

1	Kitchen
2	Living room
3	Dining deck

0   5m

While the kitchen is open to the living area, it was conceived as a module, externally clad in rosewood and stained. Elevated only millimetres above the concrete floor in the living areas, there's a sense of enclosure in the kitchen as well as connectivity. "Everything else is open to the elements," says Wolveridge, pulling back large sliding doors to the deck. To ensure the outdoors can be enjoyed at all times of the day, a second outdoor deck on the other side of the kitchen (partially covered) was included.

The kitchen comprises two-pack-painted joinery, finished in high gloss. Behind one cupboard is a fridge, and behind another cupboard are appliances and general storage. The kitchen bar appears to 'spill out' into the living area. Featuring a stone benchtop and a two-pack-painted 'lip', the bar was designed for feet to rest on the ledge.

Additional surface interest was created by including a decorative splashback in the kitchen. Wallpaper in a leafy design was inserted behind super-clear Starphire glass. Backlit, the spashback becomes a focal point.

The house is designed to take in the view of the valley and the bay

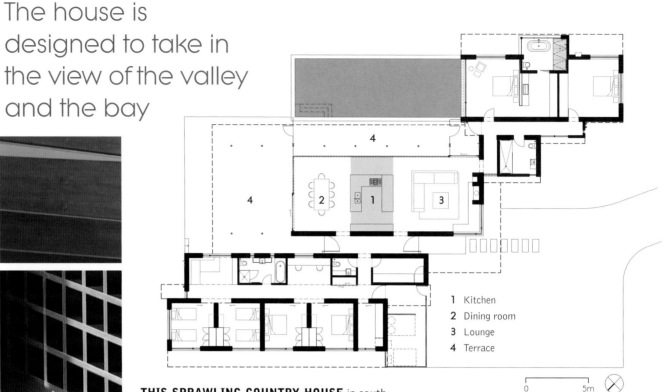

1   Kitchen
2   Dining room
3   Lounge
4   Terrace

0   5m

THIS SPRAWLING COUNTRY HOUSE in south-western Australia was designed for a British couple with four children. "They come out every year, as well as staying over at sporadic times," says architect Tim Wright, a co-director of Wright + Feldhusen Architects. "They were keen for us to draw on the local materials in the region," adds Wright.

The pavilion-style house features three wings. There are two bedroom wings (one for the children, and the other housing the main suite), and joining these two wings is an open-plan kitchen with a living area on one side and a dining or meals area on the other. "There was no need for a formal dining room. All the meals are served at the table, or around the kitchen bar," says Wright.

The house, made from stabilised limestone (rammed earth) features a U-shaped kitchen bench in the centre of the living areas. The bench is constructed from stainless steel (benchtop) with teak-veneer joinery below. The family can enjoy meals sitting at the bar or from the lounge or dining area. "The house is designed to take in the view of the valley and the bay," says Wright, who included an area for wine storage in the joinery. **>>**

The kitchen also features a bank of two-pack painted joinery. This joinery conceals a fridge, as well as a pantry. Between the two cupboards is an alcove for appliances, such as the kettle and toaster. One of the most striking features of this kitchen, is the chunky timber beams. Piercing highlight louvred-glass windows, these beams help define the spaces below. Unlike many kitchens, which feature a rectangular island bench, Wright + Feldhusen's kitchen bench is U-shaped. "It's a way of minimising through traffic, particularly with four children. This way, it's much more contained," he adds.

In keeping with the great Australian outdoors, the house includes a generous terrace and pool, giving the owners the option of eating indoors or out.

Photography credits

Index of architects and designers

240

The information and illustrations in this publication have been prepared and supplied by the participants. While all reasonable efforts have been made to source the required information and ensure accuracy, the publishers do not, under any circumstances, accept responsibility for errors, omissions and representations express or implied.